Intimate
graces

"Teresa Tomeo and Dominick Pastore have written an ingenious, engaging, wonderfully readable set of reflections on married life through the lens of the corporal works of mercy. If you're looking for a practical guide to the vocation of Christian marriage with all its joys and challenges—this is the book."

Most Rev. Charles J. Chaput, O.F.M. Cap.
Archbishop of Philadelphia

"Intimate Graces is valuable 'vocational development' for couples at every stage of the marriage life cycle."

Greg and Julie Alexander
The Alexander House

"Dominick and Teresa are offering practical, wise, and faithful lessons about marriage. The down-to-earth style will be a great help to couples who read this book."

Rev. Leo E. Patalinghug, I.V.D.
EWTN host and founder of Grace Before Meals

"In *Intimate Graces*, Teresa and Dominick invite spouses to embrace each other's humanity with all its quirks and shortcomings, to lift it up, and to heal it through the practice of the works of mercy. Rich in practical and spiritual insights, this book encourages spouses to grow in compassion for each other."

John and Teri Bosio
Creators of *Six Dates for Catholic Couples*

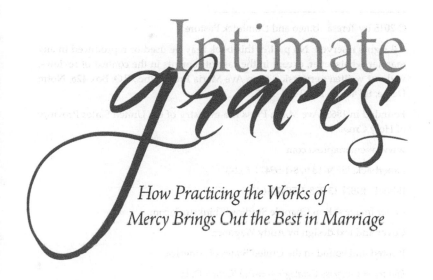

Intimate graces

How Practicing the Works of
Mercy Brings Out the Best in Marriage

Teresa Tomeo and Dominick Pastore

AVE MARIA PRESS **AVE** Notre Dame, Indiana

Unless otherwise noted, all scripture quotations are from the *New Revised Standard Version* of the Bible, © 1989 by the Division of Christian Education of the National Council of the Churches of Christ in the United States of America. Used by permission. All rights reserved.

Founded in 1865, Ave Maria Press is a ministry of the United States Province of Holy Cross.

www.avemariapress.com

Paperback: ISBN-13 978-1-59471-642-3

E-book: ISBN-13 978-1-59471-643-0

Cover image © Ron Chapple Studios/Thinkstock.com.

Cover and text design by Andy Wagoner.

Printed and bound in the United States of America.

Library of Congress Cataloging-in-Publication Data
Tomeo, Teresa.
  Intimate graces : how practicing the works of mercy brings out the best in marriage / Teresa Tomeo and Dominick Pastore.
      pages cm
  Includes bibliographical references and index.
  ISBN 978-1-59471-642-3 (alk. paper) -- ISBN 1-59471-642-0 (alk. paper)
  1. Marriage--Religious aspects--Catholic Church. 2. Church work--Catholic Church. 3. Mercy. I. Title.
  BX2250.T646 2015
  248.8'44--dc23
                                2015017826

To Heidi Hess Saxton, our wonderful editor, who gave us the idea for this book on the spiritual and corporal works of mercy that will uniquely strengthen marriages and help struggling couples to experience God's intimate graces.

Contents

Foreword by Greg and Julie Alexander......................ix

Introduction xv

One: Feed the Hungry 1

Two: Quench the Parched 11

Three: Clothe the Naked 20

Four: Shelter the Homeless 31

Five: Visit the Sick 43

Six: Ransom the Captive 52

Seven: Bury the Dead 61

Eight: Instruct the Ignorant 69

Nine: Counsel the Doubtful 77

Ten: Admonish the Sinner 86

Eleven: Bear Wrongs Patiently 97

Twelve: Forgive Offenses Willingly 107

Thirteen: Comfort the Afflicted 116

Fourteen: Pray for the Living and the Dead 126

Appendix: Resources to Help You 135

Notes 138

Foreword

Through our ministry, the Alexander House, we have been privileged to meet hundreds of couples seeking to heal, strengthen, or enrich their marriage bond. This is no small thing. The combined divorce rate in our society hovers around the 60 percent mark[1]; in addition, some experts estimate that, even among those who remain married, only 10 to 12 percent can be characterized as being "truly happy." And yet, many of these failed or struggling marriages have something in common: spouses who didn't work persistently and diligently at enriching their marriages. If you are reading this book, you are already doing something to protect and enrich your marriage . . . good for you!

Continuing education is a vital part of every vocation—doctors, attorneys, teachers, and even priests are often required to take classes and seminars to stay proficient in their fields of expertise. How many couples work as hard to build up their vocation to marriage, the most important relationship on earth?

Is it realistic to expect that we can sustain a lifetime vocation, from "I do" to "death us do part," with no more than a weekend retreat? As we minister to couples across the nation and overseas, we find that the stark reality of couples who share their aloneness is quite sad; one could even say alarming. This is truly a shame, because humans are meant to experience a foretaste of heaven, right here on earth, in and through marriage.

There are many opportunities for learning how to live a Christ-centered marriage, but we have discovered that the best way is to share the lives of those who have experienced difficulties, persevered, and made their way through the trial to rediscover the beauty in their marriages. In the words of Blessed Paul VI, "Modern man listens more willingly to witnesses than to teachers, and if he does listen to teachers, it is because they are witnesses" (*Evangelii Nuntiandi*, 41).

Intimate Graces is a beautiful example of this witness, as Deacon Dom and Teresa, along with a few other couples, share the reality of how difficult marriage can be if lived according to your design and how it can be redeemed by inviting God in and allowing the Holy Spirit to guide you through the throes of life. *Intimate Graces* is valuable "vocational development" for couples at every stage of the marriage-life cycle. Whether you are preparing for marriage, enriching an already good marriage, or looking to bring healing and resolve conflict, this book will give you hope! As they apply each of the corporal and spiritual works of mercy to married life, the Pastores have a keen way of sharing their story and transforming hearts at the same time.

Do you ever sense that you and your spouse are growing apart? Do you long to achieve the unity, the "two becoming one" that you promised in your wedding vows? Do you find yourself grappling with real-life challenges and hardships that are rocking your relationship? Or is the busyness of your life together—meeting the demands of jobs, family, and extracurricular activities—creating an unwelcome sense of separation between you? Growing together in a marriage relationship takes work, and it works when you put effort into it. If you're not sure where to begin, why not read this little book together and put these simple, intimate graces to work in your lives?

Marriage is like a plant. It is either growing, or it is dying. The only thing that is certain is it does not remain stagnant. If we do something to grow and nurture the relationship, then it will be strengthened; on the contrary, if we do nothing to strengthen or sustain our marriages, they dwindle and sooner or later are holding on for dear life.

In Hosea 4:6, the prophet says, "My people are destroyed for lack of knowledge." There is no greater lack of knowledge than for the sacrament of marriage. Saint John Paul II stated that everything travels by way of the family. Our culture, our nation—even our Church—can only be as strong as the marriages within them. When couples fail to live out God's plan for marriage, the result is devastating. But when they live and love and grow together, each person giving himself or herself 100 percent for the good of the other and for their family, it can be a foretaste of heaven on earth!

Why do we say that? Each of us received our spouse as a gift from God, to teach us to love as he loves. We are meant to give of ourselves freely and die to ourselves for the sake of the beloved. Sadly, many people want a good marriage but do not know how to get it. They have often grown up in homes that did not provide an example they desire to emulate. Many young adults today have a true fear of getting married because of what they have witnessed in their homes.

The good news is that there are specific graces we receive in the sacrament of marriage—if we cooperate with those sacramental graces the way God intended. By reading together this book, *Intimate Graces: How Practicing the Works of Mercy Brings Out the Best in Marriage*, couples will receive hope through the stories shared and practical insights into their own relationships that can transform any marriage. Allow this book to not only bring hope to your heart but also utilize the contents of this toolbox to allow your marriage to become what you never thought was possible but have dreamed could be real.

Our story is so very similar to those in this book—we are all living proof that when we incorporate the gifts of our faith (in this case, the corporal and spiritual works of mercy), God can make all things new.

Marriage was created in the Garden of Eden, with its pleasures and delights. If in your hearts you long to return to that "garden" (instead of standing on a deserted island, alone and feeling hopeless), take the first step today by entering into the depths of one another's heart as you read this book together. Open up to the grace God wants to pour out into your lives, your hearts, and your marriage. Experience heaven on earth as you assist one another in growing in holiness. Be an example for others; be a sign of Christ's love for his Church. Witness the love of God to all of those who have the opportunity to experience your example. Practice the works of mercy and bring out the best in *your* marriage!

Greg and Julie Alexander
The Alexander House

Introduction

"Everybody's got something." My husband, Dominick, and I will never forget those very simple but profound words of wisdom from a dear friend of ours, Deacon Bob Ovies from the Archdiocese of Detroit. It was more than fifteen years ago, and "Deacon Dom" and I were about to give our marriage testimony in front of more than five hundred couples at a World Marriage Day/Valentine's gathering in southeastern Michigan.

About an hour before we were to walk out the door, the phone rang. It was a friend of mine with whom I had worked in TV news for many years. She had heard about our scheduled talk and was worried about the impact my going public with so many intimate details might have on my public persona. Although I was no longer working in the secular news media, I was still on the airwaves working as a Christian talk-show host at a large FM station. I had been on the air in my hometown of Detroit, as I like to say, "since dirt," and had earned a solid reputation as a journalist.

I hung up the phone and in a panic called Deacon Bob. My friend had convinced me in a matter of minutes that everything I had worked for would come crashing down around me if we went ahead with our presentation. Deacon Bob was very involved in ministering to married couples and we had gotten to know him quite well. We trusted his opinion and knew he would be honest with us. As luck (or more likely the Holy Spirit) would have it, he was still home. That was both a surprise and a relief, since Deacon Bob and his wife, Kathy, were not only on their way to the same event but were also involved in helping with the program, so for all practical purposes they shouldn't have answered the phone.

I poured out my heart to him, sharing my friend's concerns and, quite frankly, my own second thoughts. "Maybe this isn't such a good idea after all. We don't want to leave the dinner organizers in a pinch without their keynote speakers, but maybe my friend has a point. I am a public person, after all. Is it really a good idea to let people know our most personal struggles? What if I never speak again?"

That's when I heard the three words that brought great comfort. "Everybody's got something." He went on to point out that Dom and I are hardly alone when it comes to struggling in our marriage. "You have to trust God and trust that your message will have even more impact because of the fact that you *are* a public person," he said. "Everyone thinks media personalities and others in the spotlight live perfectly charmed lives. Don't give in to fear. And again, remember—everybody's got something."

After I hung up the phone and shared what Deacon Bob had said, Dom and I took some extra deep breaths and went on to the World Marriage Day dinner. Deacon Bob was right—everybody does have something they're dealing with. Our talk was very well received. Nothing but good came of it and, quite frankly, I have lost track of how many times we've shared our marriage testimony since then, of all the ways God has transformed our lives through small, consistent acts of kindness and mercy that we have experienced within the island of mercy that is our marriage. By the mercy of God, we have come to know the intimate graces that are possible only within the safety and security of a Christ-centered marriage.

That's why I was so interested when our wonderful editor Heidi Hess Saxton approached me with this book idea based on applying the corporal and spiritual works of mercy to marriage. Although we have given our testimony on retreats, pilgrimages, marriage events, and a host of other types of gatherings—and although I have weaved our journey into my other books—it never occurred to me or my husband to write a book specifically for married couples. But thanks to Heidi (and again the Holy Spirit), here we are.

Indeed, "everybody's got something." Everybody has something in their marriage that can benefit from applying the corporal and spiritual works of mercy. That "something" in your marriage may not be in the form of a major crisis. But if we're still here on God's green earth, that means he is not through with us yet. And since we are called as husbands and wives to help get our spouses into heaven, then even the most stable of relationships can use a boost. Life happens. It certainly has its ups and downs for all of us, especially given all of the cultural attacks on marriage from the outside, not to mention the inside pressures—the busyness, the increasing demands on our time between family, work, and just the details required to get through another day. Maybe you "hunger" for deeper conversation with your spouse or a deeper faith life. This book will help you and your spouse feed the particular hunger in your marriage. Is a past sin still affecting your marriage in some way? Our chapter on burying the dead will provide encouragement to help you both move forward.

Dominick and I not only share the good, the bad, and the ugly of our own marriage journey, but we've also received input and great insights from other couples who have overcome a variety of different obstacles, big and small. Each chapter comes complete with a prayer and reflection questions. In addition, there is a resource list at the end of the book that includes our favorite ministries and websites dedicated to building and maintaining strong marriages. We hope that this book will be used in a number of different ways and settings. While it is perfect for couples to share privately, the book and study guide are also designed to be used at the parish level for marriage prep, adult catechesis, and, given the increasing role of deacons in the Church, in diaconate formation as well. We sincerely hope this will help equip future deacons to work with engaged couples and counsel couples struggling in their marriages.

"Everybody's got something." Everybody's looking for those intimate encounters with grace that can only be found in the safety and security of a Christ-centered marriage. If you are hungry to experience those graces in a new and personally transforming way, this book is for you.

One
Feed the Hungry

*Identify and respond to your partner's
deepest longings.*

For I was hungry and you gave me food ...
—Matthew 25:35

Teresa

"He doesn't understand me." "She doesn't fulfill me any longer." "I am not getting what I need from this marriage." These statements, representing a real spiritual and emotional hunger, are not just something you hear from desperate guests on the latest episode of *Dr. Phil*. Unfortunately, they are all too often spoken by many frustrated spouses.

Marriage is in crisis in our country and our world. In the United States the divorce rate still hovers around 50 to 60 percent, and the numbers aren't all that much different among those who identify themselves as Christians.

So what's the problem? How can two people who fall in love and vow to love each other "until death do us

1

part" in front of God, their family, and friends . . . then give up on their relationship just years, or in some cases, only months later?

How many other married couples, even if they're not at the breaking point, are simply going through the motions, or "going along to get along"? They're also hungry for love and acceptance—starving, actually—but are convinced that marriage is just getting through another day.

At one point in our relationship, years ago, my husband and I expressed similar feelings of disappointment and discouragement, a real emptiness and hunger. We weren't satisfied with our marriage because we didn't know what a Catholic marriage was supposed to be. When I look back on those first few years after our wedding, I could see how spiritually malnourished we really were. As Pope Francis says, too many of us fail to understand that only God can satisfy the hunger in our hearts:

"Dear friends, it is certainly necessary to give bread to the hungry—this is an act of justice. But *there is also a deeper hunger*, the hunger for a happiness that only God can satisfy, the hunger for dignity."[1]

Understanding, as Pope Francis says, that God (not a spouse) is the source of true joy and fulfillment was a real turning point for me and my husband. Dominick and I were raised Catholic and therefore married in the Catholic Church. We were, however, more catechized by the culture than by our faith. We were led to believe that the recipe for happiness equaled pursuing the American dream together. And, for a while, as we were accumulating material and professional success, the recipe tasted pretty darn good. We were, however, missing one key ingredient: God. We put him totally on the back burner, so to speak. While we still went to weekly Mass, we had no real relationship with Christ, so the recipe quickly turned sour. We fooled ourselves into thinking we were a team, but in reality it was all about pursuing personal goals and nothing about putting the other partner first.

Truly satisfying or feeding the hunger in any marriage starts with bringing Christ into the relationship and keeping him there front and center. This was beautifully expressed in a Christian billboard campaign a few years ago. Dominick and I spotted it on our way home from the airport. One of the billboards erected along major freeways across the United States spoke specifically to the issue of marriage, and, given our history, this one really hit home. It read simply, "Loved the wedding, invite me to the marriage. —God."

Okay. I know what you're thinking. That's very clever and very noble. It also sounds quite unattainable for Jane and John Q. Public. What the heck does it really mean to invite God into marriage? How in the world does it translate into the nitty-gritty of real life?

Quite frankly, it translates into a single word: self-sacrifice.

It's not a word that's often plastered on billboards or in glossy magazines; it's a word not often used to describe the prevalent cultural "me, myself, and I" lifestyle. At first glance, this idea of self-sacrifice and inviting God into the marriage doesn't make marriage seem very attractive or romantic.

Or does it?

It does if we take the time to dig a little deeper and discover the true meaning of marriage as God, not the world, ordained it. In *Familiaris Consortio,* Saint John Paul II said that at the heart of married love is the total gift of self that husband and wife freely offer to each other. "The only 'place' in which this self-giving in its whole truth is made possible is marriage, the covenant of conjugal love freely and consciously chosen, whereby man and woman accept the intimate community of life and love willed by God himself" (*FC* 11).

The United States Conference of Catholic Bishops also reminds us that marriage is a sacrament: "The bond between husband and wife is a visible sign of the sacrificial love of Christ for his Church. As a sacrament, marriage gives spouses the grace they need to love each other generously, in imitation of Christ."[2]

From the world's point of view, this "total gift of self" or "gift of sacrificial love" is seen as restrictive, oppressive, and downright medieval—straight from the Dark Ages. However, if we're talking about creating and maintaining an intimate island for your marriage, wouldn't you want to be with someone who is more than willing to give you the last slice of coconut or sip of fresh water rather than someone who has a "me first" attitude? When one spouse knows the other is doing his or her best to be more Christ-like, the relationship will be a safe haven, a real island refuge where the hunger pangs are washed away. It took us years to come to this understanding, but once we did, everything changed.

Dominick

Ever since our first date at the Gnome Restaurant in downtown Detroit, Teresa and I have enjoyed trying different foods and going to different restaurants, whether it's for a special occasion or a quick bite to eat. Our favorite, of course, is Italian, but we both enjoy a variety of cuisines. For the most part we like all the same foods except olives and avocados—I can't stand them.

However, just because we like the same foods doesn't mean that we have the same longings and desires at our deepest level. What she needs to be truly satisfied spiritually, emotionally, and intellectually is very different from what I need, and the only way we can discover what those needs are is if we share them with each other.

As an engineer (and probably also because I'm a man), I tend to see the world as a series of problems to be solved. Tell me the problem or issue and give me a little time to think about it, and I will give you a point-by-point list of how to solve it. That might be good for fixing a leaky faucet or a broken pipe, but I wouldn't recommend it as a way to truly understanding someone's deepest desires in life.

Because we are complex human beings made in the image and likeness of God, and because we live in a world that is constantly bombarding us with messages contrary to true fulfillment, it is not easy to understand our own longings, let alone someone else's.

So, how do I begin to discover what it is my spouse most needs from me—how she (or he) needs to be satisfied? Well, it starts with humility—by humbly acknowledging that I will never come to understand my wife's deepest desires on my own. Only through the power of the Holy Spirit—by listening with the ears of my heart and seeing with the eyes of Christ—can I get a glimpse into what is truly important and meaningful to my wife.

And this isn't just at those critical times in life when a crisis or major decision point comes, but—more importantly, I believe—in the everyday conversations and activities. What is she passionate about and why? What gets her up in the morning or keeps her up late at night? What are her charisms and gifts? God has made each of us for a unique purpose in his plan. Our deepest longings help reveal God's plan for our lives. To see Teresa joyful is the greatest joy in my life. To know that she is content in the Lord in whatever she is doing and in whatever is going on in her life makes me feel like I am fulfilling my marriage covenant. As a husband, my role in this matter is to help

Teresa understand and respond to her own longings and then to nurture them as best I can.

One of my favorite stories from Teresa's childhood is about the "girlie fort" (her words) that she and a few friends built in her backyard when she was about ten years old. Teresa has always been physically strong for her size, so when I first heard how she beat up the neighborhood bully who had totally wrecked their fort, I just thought it was a cute kids-being-kids type of story. It wasn't until a few years later, having come to understand the passions and desires the Lord has instilled in her, that her actions as a ten-year-old revealed not a vengeful person but one who hated injustice wherever it was found.

Through our relationship as husband and wife, as partners for the whole of life and as best friends—all under the reign of Christ—I came to understand this and respond in ways that help Teresa better realize (as in make real) her God-given passions. (So as a Christmas gift a few years ago I bought her a DVD of *The Karate Kid*. Just kidding.)

How about you? Do you want to experience this kind of intimate grace in your marriage, discovering and feeding your partner's deepest longings? For the rest of this chapter (and at the end of each chapter hereafter), we've included some tips, reflection questions, and a prayer you can offer together to set you on this journey of mutual discovery, so that you might also experience firsthand authentic intimate graces in your marriage and in your family life.

Tips for Feeding the Hunger in Your Spouse's Heart

The first corporal work of mercy, feed the hungry, has a special application within marriage for those who crave the intimacy that comes from being fully and truly known. Over time, this kind of sustained mercy and heartfelt generosity can begin to wane. It is also important to remember that just as we grow and change as individuals, so too do our needs and desires. Within marriage, it's important to share and respond generously to these changes. Below are some ways to begin this intimate journey.

Reconnect with the couple you used to be. Think back to a time in your marriage, or maybe your courtship, when sharing your deep concerns or hungers happened more easily. Recall the qualities in your spouse that made you feel so safe and comfortable. Talk about how you might be able to regain that feeling and what you can do to help each other be more open.

Look for ways to make your spouse feel safe. Sometimes we're afraid to share our deepest longings for fear of being misunderstood or even rejected by our spouse. Take some time to remind your spouse (in words and actions) that you want to help him or her address the hungers in his or her heart in order to make your marriage and your relationship with God the best it can be.

Don't be afraid of taking baby steps to reach your goal. If you are not comfortable sharing your deepest longings face to face, think about ways to begin sharing that are comfortable for you. Write a love letter or note sharing one of your desires (or asking about one of your partner's). Plan a date night in which you do something you used to enjoy doing together. Pour a glass of wine and look at old photo albums or other mementos of your courtship and talk about what you miss most about those days.

Prayer for the Hungry Heart

Lord, we know, as Saint Augustine said, that you are the only cure for our restless hearts. We know that every human longing points to a need you have placed within us to lead us closer to you. Help us guide each other along the journey of married life that will one day lead us together to experience the kind of intimate grace you want us to enjoy. Amen.

Questions for Reflection

1. What "hungers" have you noticed in your spouse's heart? How do those hungers point to unique gifts or abilities?

2. What "hungers" do you feel inside? Have you ever shared them with your spouse? If not, why not?

3. "God has made us for himself, and our hearts are restless until they rest in him" (Saint Augustine). What hungers or longings do we experience that are placed there by God and can be met only in relationship with Christ and the Church?

4. Have you discussed ways in which as a couple you can help each other, through a deeper relationship with God, satisfy the hungry heart?

Two

Quench the Parched

Partake of waters that refresh and renew your love.

‖‖

I was thirsty and you gave me something to
drink. . . .

–Matthew 25:35

Teresa

I'm a water baby. I was born on the east coast, in Jersey City,
New Jersey. My family moved to southeastern Michigan
when I was five years old. Vacations were spent out east
with my mother's family, where my grandfather would
walk me down to the docks along the Hudson River. There
were countless afternoons spent with my grandparents in
their lovely upper flat. I really enjoyed looking out their
kitchen windows at lower Manhattan and seeing the sky-
scrapers reflected in the sparkling waters surrounding
the city. Our time on the east coast often included stops
in Battery Park and Liberty Island.

As I grew up, we began to spend more time in Michigan along the beaches of the Great Lakes State. In addition to growing up near the water, my father also served for many years on the crew of the USS *United States*. His service ended before I was born, but I believe one of the reasons I love the water so very much is because I never grew tired of hearing his stories of life on the high seas. To this day—just ask my husband—no vacation is truly a vacation without at least a day or two along some body of water, large or small. I never feel quite refreshed or renewed unless I have been able to see, hear, touch, and smell water.

Even with my love of all things aquatic, I never thought much about the association between water and married love until long after we came back to the Church. As Christians, and more specifically as Christians who worship in the Catholic Church, we have most likely been taught about the importance of water when we learned about the sacrament of Baptism. We probably remember our catechist teaching us about the significance of water and its association with rebirth, sharing the story of Jesus telling Nicodemus that "no one can enter the kingdom of God without being born of water and Spirit" (Jn 3:5). Saint Peter also taught that in order for one to receive the Holy Spirit, he or she must first "repent and be baptized" (Acts 2:38).

For me, the connection between water and marriage really hit home when I began to study and read the Bible regularly. One particular chapter in scripture really helped me make the connection in terms of how we as wives and husbands are to be Christ for one another, providing that island or oasis, that place of refuge, refreshment, and complete acceptance.

In John's Gospel (4:1–30), we read the tender exchange between Jesus and the Samaritan woman at the well. The Samaritan woman has had five husbands, and when we meet her she is living with another man, not her husband. She goes to the well at high noon. Why in the world would anyone living in such a warm climate choose to go to the well when the sun is at its peak, beating down upon them?

Because everyone else would be indoors. She was hoping to avoid the cold stares and cutting comments, and this time of day was the only time for her to complete her task in peace.

Why? For starters, Samaritans were considered unclean because of their mixed heritage; Jews did not speak or mix with her kind. In addition, she was an unmarried woman living with a man, so she was not exactly up for the local Citizen of the Year award. Imagine her surprise, then, as she went to the well to quickly draw water and found a rabbi (and not just any rabbi) waiting there for her. We soon see her go from a woman ashamed to show her face in the town square to one who leaves her jug at the well and runs into that same town to tell the people about Jesus—the very people she was trying to avoid in the first place!

So what transpired between the two of them that hot sunny afternoon over two thousand years ago to prompt such a transformation in the Samaritan woman? And how does this relate to marriage? Jesus loved her exactly as she was, but as I heard one preacher say many years ago, "He loved her too much to leave her there."

And isn't that what marriage is all about—accepting our spouse's faults and loving him enough to help him reach his full potential? Because he is God, Jesus of course knew about the Samaritan woman's sordid past as well as her present circumstances. He didn't condemn her but basically told her that she deserved better and that he was the source, the living water that could quench her deep thirst and lead her to a much more meaningful and fulfilling life. And her joyful response speaks for itself: "Then the woman left her water jar and went back to the city. She said to the people, 'Come and see a man who told me everything I have ever done! He cannot be the Messiah, can he?' They left the city and were on their way to him" (Jn 4:28–30).

Now I didn't have five husbands before I met and married Dominick. But most of us, if we're honest with ourselves, will admit that in some way we are all at least a little bit like the Samaritan woman. Like the Samaritan woman, I had gotten lost in the ways of the world. I made a lot of mistakes and ignored my marriage and my other family responsibilities, all for the sake of my broadcast-journalism career. But eventually I realized—as did the Samaritan woman—that what the world had to offer left me thirsting for much more. It was my husband who offered me the living water by reintroducing me to Jesus. And just like the Samaritan woman who ran off to share the news about the man she met at the well, my greatest desire is to also serve as a witness to tell others what Christ, through my marriage, has done for me and what he can do for them, too.

Dominick

A few years ago as a Knight in the Order of Malta, I had the privilege of partaking in the order's annual pilgrimage to Lourdes in the lovely foothills of the Pyrenees Mountains in the south of France. It was my first time to Lourdes, and except for knowing that this was where the Blessed Mother appeared to Saint Bernadette as the Immaculate Conception, I didn't know much about this little town or its famous spring.

Years ago I had seen the wonderful old black-and-white film *The Song of Bernadette,* starring Jennifer Jones, about the life of this young saint. At the end of the film, Bernadette digs and digs to find the fresh spring that the Blessed Mother had told her would authenticate Bernadette's vision. It wasn't until I had actually seen this ever-flowing miraculous spring—the lifeblood of Lourdes—that I finally saw it for what it was: a lasting reminder of the love of the Word made flesh through the immaculate Virgin.

The pure, clean water of the spring flows freely all around the basilica. People from all over the world, many with severe illnesses and crippling diseases, come to bathe in this water; they drink it, bless themselves in it, and take it home with them. It is a lasting sign of Christ's love through Mary. Not everyone who visits Lourdes is cured, but everyone is healed in some way by the love that abounds throughout this very holy place.

It is this kind of love—a palpable, visible love—that continually enlivens and refreshes a marriage. It is a love born out of service for the good of the other with no ulterior motive for oneself. It often rains in Lourdes during the month that the Order of Malta makes its annual trip, but that never dampens the spirits of anyone there.

Unfortunately, the same can't be said of a marriage devoid of a Christ-centered love. The smallest of storms can cause lasting damage, and attempts at repairing the relationship are often short-lived or lack a solid foundation to build upon. If, as the *Catechism* says, the purpose of our marriage is to help each other get to heaven (see CCC 1534) and to honor the covenant that we entered into when we were married (which by its nature is ordered toward to the good of the other—see CCC 1601), then we need to pursue the selfless kind of love that flows generously from one heart to the other. We need to share each other's burdens, rejoice in the other's triumphs, and mourn the other's losses.

In the powerful 2004 film *The Passion of the Christ*, one of the most poignant scenes is when Jesus meets his mother on the road to Calvary. Beaten and bloody, he looks lovingly at Mary and says, "See, Mother? I make all things new." Through this exchange, which is based on the beautiful verse Revelation 21:5, we can begin to understand the paradox of the cross and the life-giving aspect of sacrificial love. In marriage we are renewed through this kind of love, just as Jesus and Mary are renewed—Jesus to continue his mission for the salvation of the world and Mary as the life-bearer, or *Theotokos*. They each poured out their lives unstintingly, regardless of the cost.

I aspire to love my wife this way, with a kind of love that is only possible through the sacramental grace of God. It is a love that restores and refreshes your spouse's life, and I can say that confidently because I have experienced such a love from Teresa many, many more times than I have exhibited it, and that has made all the difference.

Tips for Quenching the Parched Heart

Have you experienced this kind of self-giving love that flows from the heart of one who is fully submitted to Christ? Can you see that kind of love at work in your marriage? Or do you "thirst" for this kind of intimate grace that flows from our Baptism and is strengthened through the sacrament of Matrimony? How can the two of you strengthen these graces in your relationship? Here are some tips to consider.

Learn what the Church teaches about the purpose of marriage and the need for self-giving love. Take a closer look together as a couple at the Church's teaching on marriage (see CCC 1602–1666). Talk about what it means to you as a couple to know that your goal as a husband and wife is to help each other to heaven.

Help your spouse take a step closer to heaven this week. Think about ways you can help achieve that goal, which might include attending eucharistic adoration together or a going to Mass together during the week.

Quench your own thirst. You cannot give to your marriage what you do not have yourself. Are you spending time with God, praying and feeding on his Word? Are you taking advantage of all the graces of the sacraments and encouraging your family to do the same? What can you do this week to draw from the living water who is Christ?

Prayer for the Parched

Dear Lord, teach us to listen with the ears of our heart. Increase our sensitivity to each other's needs so that we may be able to recognize a thirst and do our best, with your guidance, to help quench that

thirst. Living Water, come and fill our hearts with
your love. Amen.

Reflection Questions

1. What does water make you think of, in the context
   of marriage? Can you think of a time you enjoyed
   together that is associated with water? Can you think
   of any water-based activities you might do together,
   as a couple, to refresh your marriage?

2. How do the other sacraments leading up to Matrimony
   plant seeds of life in us that are essential to marriage?
   What are some ways that you can, as a couple, more
   fully avail yourselves of the graces of the sacraments
   in order to fortify your marriage?

3. Take some time to read, pray about, and discuss
   together paragraphs 1534 and 1601 in the *Catechism*.

4. Did you know that the goal of marriage according to
   Church teaching is to help one's spouse get to heaven?
   What type of impact can or does this have on your
   marriage relationship?

Three

Clothe the Naked

Protect and cherish each other in vulnerable moments.

He will cover you with his pinions, and under his wings you will find refuge; his faithfulness is a shield and buckler. You will not fear the terror of the night, or the arrow that flies by day. . . .

–Psalm 91:4–5

Teresa

"Even if you decide to leave me, I won't let you leave God."

Recalling these words of my husband's as we became increasingly estranged, I can say without a doubt that Dominick "covered" me during one of the most difficult times of our lives. If he had not stuck by me, praying for me to find my way back to him and to God, today I would probably be a bitter divorced woman still covering murder stories and doing meaningless live reports on the latest snowstorm to hit the Midwest.

We are the instruments of Jesus our Savior; we are his hands and feet on this earth. My favorite saint, Teresa of Avila, reminds us that Christ "has no body on earth but yours, no hands and feet but yours." This great mystic and doctor of the Church reminds us that God wants to use us in powerful ways, yet he can do so only when we are willing to obey the Gospel mandate, "Whoever has two coats must share with anyone who has none" (Lk 3:11). Within marriage, we must stand ready to "clothe the naked," protecting and cherishing our partner even in the most vulnerable moments of life . . . including the times when, on a natural level, we would rather look away.

My husband's willingness to put his own pride aside and stick with me through thick and thin, covering me with loving and unrelenting prayer, not only saved our marriage but also gave us both a brand-new life in ministry. How does a couple close to throwing in the towel and calling the divorce lawyers end up not only writing a book about marriage but also working together in Catholic ministry? It is only by the grace of God and the willingness of one partner to lay his or her life down for the other as Christ did for each of us.

As Dominick will tell you in his own words, he was not and is not perfect. We were both to blame for our problems over the years. That said, it was my husband who refused to give up. That's because God had come back into his life and grounded him, enabling him to stick with it. His faith also gave him insight as to why I was sinking deeper and deeper into the captivity of worldliness. When God allowed a professional crisis to occur in my life, Dom was there to throw me a life preserver, and that's when the changes in my own life began.

The broadcast news business is almost as competitive and cutthroat as Hollywood or Broadway. It's a "take-no-prisoners," everyone-for-themselves atmosphere. The media often do exposés on companies who mistreat their employees, and yet that is a regular occurrence in newsrooms. You're only as good as your last story, and if you're not willing to work the extra hours and yet one more weekend or holiday shift, then they will remind you that they can quickly find someone younger and cheaper to take your place. And forget about putting family first.

Despite all the talk of fair labor practices, there is no such thing in newsrooms. Wanting to see your loved ones during reasonable hours can inhibit job advancement: if you set those kinds of personal boundaries publicly, you can pretty much kiss any chance of the promotion to the anchor desk goodbye. This is becoming the norm not only in the news business but in other demanding fields as well. Former State Department employee and lawyer Anne-Marie Slaughter wrote openly about this in the June 13, 2012, cover story in *The Atlantic* titled "Why Women Still Can't Have It All."[1] She was practically tarred and feathered by radical feminists.

It took my losing a very prominent position in TV news to begin the detox process. The job loss literally happened overnight. My contract was up for renewal and given that the ratings at the TV station were not going as well as anticipated, management decided that they needed some on-air changes. I was one of them, along with several other reporters and anchors working at the time.

I can remember walking out of the newsroom with my box of belongings and thinking, *All the sacrifices I had made, and for what?* I had chosen the job over my marriage so many times, and this was the thanks I was getting? Nothing more than a severance check and a humbling place on the unemployment line? I had been so caught up in being the successful career woman, believing the lies that the world tells women: your job comes first. Everything else is secondary. I was taught that if I worked hard I would be rewarded, not tossed out with the garbage like yesterday's newspaper.

Thanks be to God, Dominick was home, waiting to wrap me up in his loving arms. Oh, I didn't have a "come to Jesus" moment right away. My ego was too battered and bruised to think about much more than getting through another day of not being on the air—something I had been doing since I was a teenager. But after months of butting heads with God and ignoring my husband's patient pleas to reconsider our Catholic faith, I said "uncle." I stopped seeing God as my copilot or passenger on my private plane and told Jesus to take the wheel.

The changes in our relationship were gradual. There were a lot of ups and downs as I attempted to take back the wheel, but somehow we stayed on course despite some pretty big potholes and traffic jams. I began to see that while it was perfectly fine to have a successful career and do what we love, no career can replace God and family. If we put our trust in the world, the world will surely disappoint. I also learned another important lesson that I hope I will never forget.

In marriage we are called to "die to self"—to be completely open and vulnerable with one another physically, emotionally, and spiritually. In marriage, we are called to be "one," without shame and without reservations. We are called . . . to be naked, for that is the only way to know what it is to be protected and cherished.

At the same time, we are called to protect and cherish . . . for that is the only way that our spouse's heart can be truly open to us, so that we might be fully one. And when we allow ourselves to love in that way—vulnerable and cherished, naked and unashamed—we will find a peace that surpasses all understanding and a deeper joy than we could ever imagine.

With the help of an incredibly merciful and loving God, that's what Dominick did for me and for our relationship. He "covered" me at my most vulnerable time and brought me back to God, and God gave us a new life and a new marriage.

Dominick

"If you don't have anything nice to say, don't say anything at all." "You're just like your father." "Well . . . You're just like your mother." These were not uncommon tête-à-têtes between me and Teresa when we were first married. I was too impatient, like my dad, and she was too bossy, like her mother.

For better or worse, we are greatly shaped by our past: our family upbringing, schooling, and life experiences. Our past can add very beautiful aspects to our marriage. For example, one of my family traditions is the Christmas Eve dinner with a variety of different fish dishes, pastas, and delicious Italian desserts. Although Teresa is also Italian American, she never had that tradition growing up. After we were married we made an effort to try to bring that into our Christmas celebration with her family. Happily, it has become an event that everyone looks forward to.

On the other hand, we all carry a lot of baggage into our marriages. Often that baggage doesn't really begin to get unpacked until well after the honeymoon, even if a couple is engaged for a long time (Teresa and I were engaged almost three years). We sometimes-frail human beings are pretty good at being on our best behavior until after we walk down the aisle. It's not that we purposely hide our past from the other person, but it is a natural tendency to diminish those things that make us seem less attractive, if we are aware of those weaknesses at all. Some flaws come to light only in the most intimate relationships of marriage.

Teresa is an extrovert and I am an introvert. For a good part of my life the word "introvert" was like a four-letter word. I hated that characteristic of my personality. When Teresa and I were together, alone, I think it helped us to be more private and introspective with each other; on the other hand, it became a difficult issue for her and sometimes for me in public, especially at media-related events that were saturated with "uber extraverts." This kind of atmosphere made me want to withdraw, creating resentment on Teresa's part and more self-loathing on my part. This led to a destructive cycle of non-communication; often I didn't feel like Teresa loved me for who I was. Teresa has other, similar stories to tell about me, I'm sure.

I've learned that it takes a long time to really get to know someone, to let down those protective outer layers in order to be truly vulnerable and open with another person—and to let the one I love do the same. That is the true blessing of marriage, to have that one other person in the world you can discover in a new way, each and every day, and to reveal a bit more of yourself without fear. If you are blessed in your marriage in this way, there will be new wonderful things to learn about the other person every day.

When we are able to do this, we reflect in a small way the open communion that is the life-giving love of the Blessed Trinity. We know this because we see it in many of the one-on-one conversations Jesus had with people in scripture; it's never a superficial exchange (though at times those who are listening don't completely understand him). Whether it is Nicodemus asking what it means to be born again, the woman at the well, the woman caught in adultery, or even Pilate ("What is truth?"), Jesus plumbs the depth of the soul to bring out and offer healing and freedom of both body and soul to those who were willing to expose their hearts to him. As Jesus did, so am I to do.

Jesus never condemned those who came to him because of past sins; instead he offered forgiveness and healing for a life freed of the past. Similarly, my role as a husband is to commit myself to clothing the one I love in grace, becoming a patient and understanding vehicle for healing and acceptance. I cannot force her to uncover her heart; I can only cherish and protect her, to show her it is safe. And she does the same for me.

The love that we have for one another, the intimacy that we share, the freedom we allow for the other to feel safe, and the trust that we have knowing that our past will never be a weapon used against us are the Christlike qualities I must manifest to my wife.

Tips to Protect the Vulnerable Heart

In Paul's letter to the Colossians, we are told to "clothe" ourselves in the virtues that are at the heart of all authentic love, the first buds of the fruit that the Spirit works within us as we perform these works of mercy:

> As God's chosen ones, holy and beloved,
> clothe yourselves with compassion, kind-
> ness, humility, meekness, and patience.
> Bear with one another and, if anyone has
> a complaint against another, forgive each
> other; just as the Lord has forgiven you, so
> you also must forgive. (Col 3:12–13)

Within your own marriage, do you see this "clothing" work in action? Let's take a look at some things you can do to strengthen this habit of mercy in your relationship.

Choose to be vulnerable with each other. Sometimes we don't open ourselves up completely to our spouse because we are afraid of being judged, hurt, or embarrassed. With these concerns in mind, sit down together and promise each other you will protect that vulnerability.

Affirm your spouse for the ways he or she has "covered your nakedness" in the past. Discuss a time in your relationship when you believe your spouse helped you move past a particularly sensitive issue or experience. Share how that made you feel.

Refuse to "uncover" a spouse to the outside world. In difficult times it can be tempting to vent grievances about a spouse to the sympathetic ear of a close friend or family member. And yet, this can also do great damage to the intimate space of a marriage. Consider talking to a priest or counselor if you need a fresh perspective. Ask forgiveness if you have "exposed" your partner's weaknesses, and work to rebuild that trust.

|||||||||||||||||||||||||||||||||||||||||||||||||||||||||||||||||||||||||||||||||||||||||||||||||||||||||||||||||||||||||||||||||||||||||||||||||||||||||

Prayer for the Vulnerable Heart

Dear Lord, help us to cherish and protect one another, even at our most vulnerable and frightened. Forgive us for the ways we have failed to "cover" each other, and help us to grow in trust for each other as together we grow closer to you, the sweet Redeemer, the one who truly sets us free. Amen.

|||||||||||||||||||||||||||||||||||||||||||||||||||||||||||||||||||||||||||||||||||||||||||||||||||||||||||||||||||||||||||||||||||||||||||||||||||||||||

Reflection Questions

1. Think of a time in your past—during your marriage or even before you met—that you felt exposed to the world and in need of protection. How does recalling that memory make you feel today? Pray together that God would show you how to protect and cherish one another, and to help one another to find healing from the past.

2. What kind of "nakedness" is most difficult for you? What are some ways that you've tried to "cover" your own nakedness in the past? In what ways has marriage "clothed" you?

3. Read the Colossians 3:12–13 passage again. When you look at your spouse, which of these qualities do you think "fit" him (or her) best? Which of these would you like to grow in?

4. In marriage we experience a foretaste of what it is to be "known" by God. How does this make you feel? Tell God about it. He wants to hear your thoughts and to "cover" you with his love and mercy.

Four

Shelter the Homeless

Become "home" for the one you love.

||||||||||||||||||||||||||||||||||||||||||||||||||||||||||||||||||||||||||||||||||||||||||||||||||||||||||||||||

> Now as they went on their way, he entered a
> certain village, where a woman named Martha
> welcomed him into her home.
>
> *–Luke 10:38*

Teresa

As Dorothy told Auntie Em in *The Wizard of Oz*, "There really is no place like home." That saying brings warm fuzzies to most fans of this classic movie. After her crazy trip to and from Oz—complete with lions, tigers, bears, and wicked witches—Dorothy is grateful to be back in the sleepy Kansas countryside. She is welcomed with open, loving arms by family and friends. And they all lived happily ever after. Toto too!

But that's Hollywood fiction, and this is real life. So if your marriage situation looks more like the haunted forest than Dorothy's farmhouse, home might be the last place you want to be. Or, if you've reached a place in your

relationship where you simply miss the music and color
of the dream, where do you begin to restore the life and
harmony that once characterized your life together?

That may sound a bit melodramatic, but if you have
ever lived through a difficult time in a marriage because
of the stressors each of you brought home with you, you
no doubt get the analogy.

Many of us support local homeless shelters with our
time or money. In my days as a secular news reporter I covered a lot of stories involving serving the needy, in particular around the holidays. That's because we see how much
difference these shelters make. Even short-term care gives
the homeless a chance to regroup in a safe environment
away from the cold, mean streets. There is no judgment
or condemnation. All are welcome.

Ironically, it is sometimes easier to help strangers in
need of comfort than to provide spiritual and emotional
help to our life's partner, or to make our home at least
as safe as the local shelter down the street. How can we
begin to create an "island of mercy," a space in which
each of us has the same feeling Dorothy did when she
woke up to find herself back in familiar and comfortable
surroundings?

For Dominick and me, it was a case of the old "which
came first: the chicken or the egg?" Our opposite personalities were what initially attracted us to each other, but
as we got older those same personalities began to clash
all too regularly. Dom is as solid as a rock, and everyone

in the family goes to him for advice. His caring and gentle personality draws people to him and makes him less likely to talk about himself and to always put others first. That's why I always knew, when he first told me that he was discerning the call to the diaconate, that he would be so good at ministry—he has such a sacrificial and Christlike demeanor about him.

During the early years of our marriage, I relied on Dom to help me navigate the stormy waters of the very competitive and demanding news business. He always had great advice. I just didn't know when to quit, and I didn't think to ask him very often what he might be experiencing as he moved up the corporate ladder at his engineering firm. He either didn't say much, or I didn't ask. We both needed to do a better job of communicating with one another. I needed to do a little *less* communicating, and he needed to do *more*.

Because of our lack of understanding of what the other person needed, little things became bigger than they needed to be. Domestic chores and money were just two of the issues that could spark a fire and lead to more distance between us. Add to that two very busy work schedules, and you have a recipe for disaster.

Our problems left Dominick with a longing for something deeper in his life and in our marriage. Overall I was thrilled with the levels of success we were both achieving in the career world, but I became increasingly frustrated by the tensions at home. I had figured our marriage would take care of itself, and it didn't occur to me that we needed anything more than time. All that began to change when Dominick was invited to a men's Bible study at church and he experienced a powerful sense of conversion. In his zeal, he became determined to win me back to the faith as well.

Unfortunately, Dominick's first attempts were somewhat heavy-handed; instead of bringing me closer to Jesus and to him, they pushed me away. I didn't feel safe, because I felt that I was being judged for not being Christian enough for my husband. I felt as if I didn't measure up to his spiritual standards. I later realized that, although my husband could have approached me in a less zealous manner, deep down the Holy Spirit was convicting me. I didn't want to admit what I already knew: even though I considered myself a Catholic, I was not practicing my faith. For the most part, I had turned into a Christmas-and-Easter Christian.

Dominick's involvement with the men's Bible study program quickly blossomed into much more involvement at our parish, along with classes at Sacred Heart Major Seminary in Detroit. His newfound faith would eventually be the glue that held us together at the most difficult of times, and paved the way for a new beginning and better understanding of what it means to provide shelter in marriage. For a while his faith made me uncomfortable, though in time it was to become a channel of transforming grace.

As spouses, we can begin to become an "island of mercy" for one another—a place of intimate grace, safety, and belonging—simply by paying more attention to one another when we are at home. For me and Dom, that meant we both had to give a little. I had to resist the temptation to talk nonstop about work as well as to say at least an occasional "no" when the assignment desk called asking me to cover a breaking news story or another weekend shift. For Dom's part, he had to learn to express his needs and concerns and gently remind me when I was allowing shop talk to dominate our conversation. We learned some of this on our own and some of it through the great experience we had at a Marriage Encounter weekend. There we were reminded of some of the things we do as couples that inadvertently break down that sense of belonging and security.

Dominick

I'm blessed. My best friend and closest confidant—the one who knows more about me than any other person, the one I feel most at home with—also happens to be my wife. There is no place in my life as secure, safe, and comfortable as in the companionship of Teresa. But it wasn't always that way.

Teresa and I are about as opposite as two people can get. She is very outgoing and full of life; I'm quiet and private with my feelings and emotions. As an engineer, I'm very practical and results-oriented; Teresa is a free thinker who, shall we say, definitely likes to color outside the lines.

Our opposite qualities were one of the things that attracted us to each other when we first met; our different likes and dislikes were fun and interesting to explore and experience. Life was an adventure. As we "settled in" to married life—without a strong understanding of our faith and thus an equally weak concept of marriage—these differences soon went from uniquely charming to intensely irritating. Did I really need to hear about all the drama at her workplace again? The solution to the problem was simple: just do this and that and problem solved. Why couldn't Teresa load the dishwasher in an organized fashion—cups on one side, plates on the other—so that we could get in the maximum amount of dishes? It didn't take long to go from opposites attracting to opposites attacking. The only solution—or so we thought—was to turn the other person into someone like our self, and the harder we tried the worse it got.

Home was no longer a happy, peaceful place but one of tension and conflict. Sometimes just making it through a weekend without some kind of incident was a major accomplishment. Often, no matter how stressful work was, it was a more of a home than home was. At home we would say things to each other that were deliberately intended to be hurtful and, sad to say, things that were shared long ago in deep confidence were now being used as ammunition to win an argument or prove a point.

"All have sinned and fall short of the glory of God" (Rom 3:23). Yes, Saint Paul says "all," and when this scripture passage finally sunk in, I realized I wasn't all that I thought I was. I hadn't done my part—regardless of what Teresa may or may not have been doing—to make our marriage a place of love and harmony. Being not that bad of a husband and better than most (from what I saw in the world) was not nearly enough.

What I came to realize is that as a husband I needed to be that person whom Teresa can totally rely on, be comfortable with, be herself with—in short, that person who protects, shelters, allows to grow, and honors who she is as a person created in the image and likeness of God. None of that is possible without loving unconditionally (to the best of my ability) and forgiving quickly. At first it was difficult—for both of us—not to trade barbs. It's not easy to return good for evil; only by personally knowing the love and forgiveness that Jesus gives me every single day is it possible to share that with my wife.

Several years ago, during our first trip to Italy, Teresa and I were walking down one of the side streets of Rome, near the Pantheon. On one side of the street were mostly restaurants full of people eating outside; on the other there were mostly shops, almost everyone speaking Italian (of which we could understand none). For some reason we both had the same feeling at the same time. I think it was Teresa who spoke first—not an uncommon occurrence in our marriage—when she said something like, "Don't you feel really comfortable here, almost at home?" I did.

I'm reminded of that experience when I think of what it means to be "home" for the other person. As we walk along the path of life, within the familiar yet amid uncertainties, when you don't understand all that is happening around you, whether in times of stress or not, my role as a husband is to nurture in Teresa a sense of peace and trust, a quietness of spirit so that together we can continue on our journey. Obviously, our true peace and safe haven comes from Jesus, but if I'm not modeling that and being a conduit for Christ's peace and joy to my wife, then I'm not being the husband I need to be. Walking down that street in Rome, there was both a familiarity (because of our Italian heritage) and a newness (maybe with some anxiety being in a foreign land) to the experience. Isn't that the case with most of our experiences as husband and wife: whether difficult and trying or happy and joyful, there is something that is different, but there is a foundation that your wife can rely on—Christ most assuredly, without fail—but you, too, if you're being the "builder" husband God created you to be.

Tips for Sheltering the One You Love

Have you fallen for the myth of "quality time"? One of the biggest issues for couples today is the mistaken notion that as long as they are physically in the house together, that qualifies as quality time. Don't buy it. As we minister together to couples around the country, husbands and wives come up to tell us how alone they feel, even when their spouse is sitting in the same room. Why? Because when they are together, their husband or wife is focusing their attention on the TV or computer screen. Here are a few practical issues to consider as you begin to take steps toward making your marriage the kind of "home" each of you needs.

Make sure electronics aren't short-circuiting your marriage. A study released in the summer of 2014 confirms why so many spouses feel anything but sheltered and loved at home. Too many men and women would prefer to spend time with their favorite media outlet or gadget than their own loved ones. The study found that adults prefer to watch their favorite programs alone in another room even if other family members are home with them—a sad case of being together but so alone and far apart. As you evaluate your home life, consider what you might do to "unplug" in order to connect with greater intimacy. For some, it might simply be a matter of getting in the habit of walking outside together after dinner; others might decide to remove electronics from the bedroom for the sake of a better night's sleep . . . and a more intimate personal connection at the end of the day.

Appreciate the "sound of silence." This is related to the last point. Scripture tells us that God comes to us in the silence—both interior and exterior. If we don't provide a peaceful environment at home, we won't be able to hear what God has to say to us as a married couple. Instead of having your husband or wife greeted by the blare of *Lifetime* television or even Catholic radio, why not greet him or her with open arms and the warmth of your voice? If you are longing for your home to be a less hectic place, stop and take a closer look at your list of outside activities and commitments. Is there something you can give up that would allow you to be home, say, even one additional night a week? These seem like small steps, but we found little gestures of dying to self eventually lead to a real change.

Are you and your spouse in different places, spiritually speaking? If you find yourself right now on the faith fast track, don't try to force your spouse to get behind the wheel. Pray. Invite her to attend Mass with you and once in a while to a church event, then let her be and pray some more. The more you pray, the more peaceful you will be. It was the peace that Dominick had that finally won Teresa over.

Take steps to avoid a "spiritual shipwreck." If you have more serious issues in your marriage—such as abuse, addiction, or infidelity—it is probably time to seek counseling and/or the help of a priest or spiritual director. It would be wonderful if we had our own version of Glenda the Good Witch to make everything all right again. But down here on planet Earth, it takes a lot more than waving a magic wand or clicking heels to right the wrongs and heal the wounds in our lives.

Love one another. Look out for one another. Make time for one another. Be a little like Dorothy and a lot like Jesus. And pretty soon you, too, will be telling your spouse the same thing Dorothy told Auntie Em: "If I ever go looking for my heart's desire, I won't go looking any further than my own backyard. Because . . . I never lost it in the first place." Home is indeed where the heart is, and where your hearts should be.

Prayer of the Sheltered Heart

Dear Lord, help us be more like your Holy Family by keeping our home a safe and loving place. May we grow and love together, loving and protecting each other. May all who enter here feel truly welcome and believe we see them as a treasured gift from you. Amen.

Reflection Questions

1. When I think of the word "home," what image comes to mind? How does my spouse fit into this image? For parents with children at home: How does our marriage make our children feel more "at home"?

2. What am I doing right now, as a spouse, to be "home" for the one I love? What could I do to reconnect with my spouse better when we see each other at the end of the day?

3. What could I be doing in our home life in terms of extracurricular activities and media consumption that could help bring us closer? As a couple, do we need to look at outside help in order to heal the hurts?

4. Because God created marriage to be an earthly expression of divine love, he wants to be part of your marriage. Do you experience Christ and his Church to be "home" for your family? How can you strengthen this connection?

Five

Visit the Sick

Bring a healing touch to those who suffer.

||||||||||||||||||||||||||||||||||||||||||||||||||||||||||||||||||||||||||||||||||||||||||||||||||||||||||||||||||||||||||||||||||||||||||||||||||||||||||||||||||||||||||||||||

> Therefore confess your sins to one another, and
> pray for one another, so that you may be healed.
> The prayer of the righteous is powerful and
> effective.
>
> *–James 5:16*

Teresa

"Don't you understand that your father was helping me get to heaven?" It was shortly after my father passed away on the feast of Our Lady of Sorrows, September 15, 2010, that my mother uttered these profound words filled not only with love but also with solid Catholic teaching.

She posed the question after I was telling her how concerned I was about her own health. About two months before my father died, Mom finally agreed to get some in-home help; this after several years of being the primary caregiver for my father, who struggled with Parkinson's disease and a heart condition. This meant helping him get dressed in the morning, helping him bathe, and doing all of the meal preparation. At the time of my father's death, my mother was eighty-four years old. Arthritis was starting to take its toll on her strength and balance, and Dominick and I were grateful that she finally allowed an aide to handle *some* of my father's care. I said to my mom that I was really worried that if she continued all of the care by herself that, God forbid, I would lose both of them in a very short period of time.

Although my mom never went to Catholic school or studied theology, her words hit the nail on the head: "Don't you understand that your father was helping me get to heaven?" With that one question, she managed to summarize what the sacrament of marriage is all about. She looked at me as if I had lost my mind. Here I was the Catholic talk-show host, speaker, and author. What was I thinking? Didn't I know this was her way of living out her marriage vows?

I don't know if Mom could cite the actual *Catechism* references concerning the meaning of marriage, but she certainly lived the faith during her nearly six decades of being a wife and mother. If the sacrament of marriage, as the *Catechism* reminds us, is indeed ordered for the good of the other person, then what better example could there be than a spouse "visiting" the one she loves even in his sufferings, standing by to soothe the suffering with a touch like a healing balm?

Only in this context of such an intimate family relationship is this kind of "visitation" possible: for better or worse, whether at dawn or midnight, this constant presence can provide a kind of healing and comfort like no other. And in pouring out ourselves and binding ourselves more intimately to one another, we experience a taste of heaven here and now—and draw closer to the eternal joys of heaven, step by step, as we attain holiness through these selfless acts of service.

For my mom, serving her husband was one of the important ways she lived out her commitment to God. She has always taken her faith seriously, never missing Mass except for illness. She was also involved in a number of faith-related activities, including a weekly women's prayer group. But she was also head-over-heels in love with my father (and vice versa). In all my years, I never heard my father call my mother by her first name; it was always a term of endearment, usually "honey" or "hon." He referred to her in conversation with others as Rose or Rosie, but in direct conversation it was again always a term of endearment. Mom also told me in that same very blunt conversation we had while planning Dad's funeral that if she had died in the process of providing loving care for my father, it would have been a blessing and an honor.

What a contrast to what we see and hear in our world today! I'm sure we all know people in our circles with similar stories of commitment and sacrifice. Unfortunately, these stories of love, fidelity, mercy, and commitment often don't make the headlines, the latest Facebook feeds, or the blogosphere. Those who take the opposite approach to the sick and suffering garner much of the attention. They're praised for being brave and are even called heroes in many cases. While only God can judge a person's heart, what is heroic or brave about giving up? The real heroes are those who are willing to live up to their commitments and those well-known words recited at each wedding ceremony: *in sickness and in health*. Real bravery is the willingness to not only visit but also care for the sick. In the end, we not only help the other person, but we help ourselves immensely as well.

Dominick

"In sickness and in health, till death do us part." We've probably all heard these words at numerous weddings. But how many of us, whether at our own wedding or in the course of married life, really think about the implications of this part of our marriage vows? We might think about it in terms of, say, a common type of sickness such as the flu or an attack of appendicitis. But unless you have experienced a life-changing illness or disease, it may be hard to get your head around those actual words.

At age forty-one my father suffered an acute heart attack. This began a battle with heart disease that lasted half his lifetime, until he died at the age of eighty-two. During that time, my dad's medical history included a long list of heart-related ailments and treatments: he had close to a dozen heart attacks of various degrees, three open-heart surgeries, several angioplasties, two stints, and one experimental heart procedure. He had more trips to emergency room than you could count. Ultimately, blood cancer took his life.

The only thing greater than my dad's courage was my mom's loving service and her rising above the expected to do the exceptional: purposely driving down one-way streets the wrong way to get my dad to the hospital quickly, countless hours spent by his side in the hospital, cleaning up his biological accidents toward the end of his life—all while raising a family. My dad was never an invalid until the last few months of his life, but without my mom there, he would have never lived the wonderful life he had. They had their moments, to be sure, but that never clouded their love for one another.

Being a caretaker (or care receiver) is seldom easy or enjoyable. It means submitting ourselves to the desires and needs of another person, not for selfish gain but out of necessity or loss of autonomy. It is a life Saint Peter knew, as Jesus foretold in John's Gospel when he told him, "But when you grow old, you will stretch out your hands, and someone else will fasten a belt around you and take you where you do not wish to go" (Jn 21:18; see also verse 19). Although Peter's way was a product of persecution because of his beliefs, the personal dynamics are very similar—giving up oneself out of love for another (i.e., Jesus) so that the other can live more abundantly (as the

Gospel lives more abundantly throughout the world). This is the fabric of a faith-filled life of service, in "visiting the sick." Even at our weakest moments, we have the humility to allow ourselves to be ministered to or to minister to another.

Maybe it's our pride or perhaps it's our American individualism, but regardless, we want to be in control of our lives. However, we have been bought with a price, and the life we live is no longer ours—it is Christ living within us (see Gal 2:20). Teresa and I both feel so blessed that we have such wonderful examples of this to imitate, as each day we love each other "in sickness and in health," just as our parents did throughout their many years of marriage.

Tips for "Visiting" a Sick Loved One

Whether an illness is minor and fleeting, serious and chronic, physical or emotional or spiritual, the suffering of a spouse presents a unique opportunity to affirm the marriage commitment and grow in more perfect love. How can you put this corporal work of mercy to better use in your relationship?

Consider the past. Take some time out with your spouse and reflect upon how your partner has put this particular corporal work of mercy into practice. Recall how it made you feel when the love of your life made the effort to truly visit you when you were sick. Remember that sometimes our illnesses manifest themselves spiritually or emotionally as well as physically. Look for ways to return the favor.

Prepare in the present. What can you do to prepare for your "visit" now, before it happens? Is your hall closet or medicine chest stocked with whatever you might need? (If you have children and your partner is the regular caregiver, consider creating a "survival plan" for the days you need to take over.) Have you made an advance directive and made important papers and account numbers readily accessible, in case of true emergency, to prevent unnecessary anxiety for your spouse?

Look to the future. In times of illness, one of the best gifts we can offer our spouse is the gift of hopeful perspective. Each Good Friday is one step closer to the glory of Easter. Each humble, unremarkable act of service is an offering of perfect love when we look at it from the perspective of heaven. When we "take up our cross" and follow a spouse in times of suffering, we can imitate Saint Veronica and Saint Simon of Cyrene, who served the Savior in his hour of need.

Prayer for Those
Who Struggle with Illness

Pray this portion of what's known as "The Prayer
of Saint Francis" together as a couple. Ask the Lord
to help you deepen your understanding of what it
means to visit the sick in your marriage.

> O Divine Master, grant that I may not so
>   much seek
> To be consoled as to console;
> To be understood as to understand;
> To be loved as to love.
> For it is in giving that we receive;
> It is in pardoning that we are pardoned;
> And it is in dying that we are born
>   to eternal life.
> Amen.

Reflection Questions

1. Can you think of stories within your extended family, examples of spouses who "visited the sick" and strengthened their marriage in times of physical or

emotional suffering? What did they teach you about loving "in sickness and in health"?

2. What are some of the most personally meaningful gestures you have ever received when you've been sick? What kinds of "visits" are most frustrating or difficult?

3. The illness or disability of extended family members can also present great challenges to a married couple. What do you think it means to "honor your father and mother" if an elderly parent or relative is in need of care? Have you talked about—and agreed upon—what you will do if this happens?

4. Being a caregiver of a chronically ill spouse can be a heavy cross as well as an opportunity to be "love in action." What are some important ways to keep life in balance during times of illness? Are there any areas of your life you need to work on so you both remain as healthy as possible for as long as possible?

Six

Ransom the Captive

Allow God to capture our hearts.

||||||||||||||||||||||||||||||||||||||||||||||||||||||||||||||||||||||||||||||||||||||||||||||||||||||||||||||||||||||||||||

When [the servant-girl] saw Peter warming himself, she stared at him and said, "You also were with Jesus, the man from Nazareth." But he denied it, saying, "I do not know or understand what you are talking about." And he went out into the forecourt. Then the cock crowed. And the servant-girl, on seeing him, began again to say to the bystanders, "This man is one of them." But again he denied it. Then after a little while the bystanders again said to Peter, "Certainly you are one of them; for you are a Galilean." But he began to curse, and he swore an oath, "I do not know this man you are talking about." At that moment the cock crowed for the second time. Then Peter remembered that Jesus had said to him, "Before the cock crows twice, you will deny me three times." And he broke down and wept.

–Mark 14:67–72

Teresa

In the Old City of Jerusalem there is a beautiful Catholic church associated with Saint Peter's betrayal of Jesus on Holy Thursday. Saint Peter in Gallicantu (*gallicantu* means "cock crows" in Latin) is one of my favorites in all of the Holy Land. This church is filled with brilliantly colored and hauntingly moving mosaics depicting this powerful scene from the Gospels. In one mosaic panel we can clearly see the love and sadness pouring out of the Lord's eyes and the immediate remorse exuding from Saint Peter's after the apostle utters those infamous words: "I do not know him."

You might be wondering why someone would find a church that is a reminder of such a painful part of the first pope's life to be among their favorite pilgrimage sites. The reason is quite frankly because, as Paul Harvey used to say, we know "the rest of the story." It's a story that reminds us of our own journey of redemption. It is a story that reminds me of how my husband ransomed this captive from herself and showed her the difference between remorse and condemnation, the same way that Christ revealed his forgiveness and mercy to Saint Peter after the Resurrection along the seashore, the place marked today by the Church of the Primacy of Saint Peter.

How does this relate to my story? Girls and young women growing up in the 1970s were presented with unprecedented opportunities. We were told by the feminists of the day, such as Betty Friedan and Gloria Steinem, that we could "have it all."

They lied. And countless women bought into the lie, as did countless men. Dominick and I were no exception to the rule. The world in which we lived said women and men could have it all and should have it all. So off we went from the "hear us roar" '70s smack dab into the young urban professional, or "yuppie," mentality of the '80s, never stopping along the way to think about the path we were taking until it was almost too late.

Dominick was the first one to sense something was rotten in Denmark. Despite all of the success, he felt something was missing in our lives and in our marriage. We were accumulating lots of stuff and earning lots of money, but we were never really together enough to enjoy it.

A year later, all that changed when I lost my job and found myself in the unemployment line. The TV station had made some changes, and I happened to be one of them. That wasn't unusual for the very unstable business of broadcast news, but I wasn't prepared for it. It turned out, however, to be the best thing that ever happened to me.

The unemployment line can be a pretty long and pretty darn lonely one, giving one a lot of time to reflect. The months off forced me to take a good long look at myself and realize that I needed to do what my husband had done: take our faith and our relationship much more seriously. For far too long I had just thought our marriage would take care of itself.

Through years of ups and downs and lots of long, drawn-out and very heated discussions with the Lord, with counselors, and with each other we were finally able to heal our marriage. But the role I played in our problems haunted me for many years. It took a lot of love, prayer, patience, and positive reinforcement from my husband to convince me that I was truly worthy of his and God's love.

Still, I remained a "captive" in a very real sense of the word. I was so ashamed of how poorly I had treated my husband, how I was so quick to run out the door to cover the next hot breaking news story or run as fast as I could to the latest and greatest social function of the season. The prophet Jeremiah proclaimed God's intention:

> When you search for me, you will find me;
> if you seek me with all your heart, I will
> let you find me, says the Lord, and I will
> restore your fortunes and gather you from
> all the nations and all the places where I
> have driven you, says the Lord, and I will
> bring you back to the place from which I
> sent you into exile. (29:13–14)

If we're really seeking God, he will show us some things about ourselves that will be tough to face—not for our condemnation but for our growth and our good. He wants to "gather us" and "bring us back" from exile and return us to the place it all began . . . to a kind of Eden, a place of intimate grace and healing love. He wants to ransom our captive hearts and help us experience the freedom of his abundant mercy and love.

The alternative is not a pretty one. Whereas Peter reconciled with the Lord and experienced that abundant healing and forgiveness, Judas turned in on himself and away from that source of grace. He couldn't look at himself or live with himself, so he took his own life. However, we see Saint Peter dramatically change from a despondent and ashamed man sitting by a charcoal fire in Jerusalem to a redeemed man sitting by another charcoal fire along the Galilean seashore, now looking lovingly and oh-so-gratefully at the risen Christ.

His story reminds us of an important truth: we can't let go of our past until we confront it honestly. That's what Jesus did for Saint Peter. That's what Dominick, through Jesus, did for me.

Dominick

Several years ago I attended a business-management seminar. One of the key points the presenter made was that for a company to grow leaders, they need not only to understand each other's strengths and weakness but also to trust one another. By building up a sense of trust in the group, the fear of failure is minimized, which in turn facilitates personal and corporate growth.

The same is true for marriage. When we as husband and wife trust each other with life and soul, fear is driven out and our marriages can flourish. When we have each other's back, I'm not afraid to challenge myself to be the best husband I can be. Saint John stated all of this in his first epistle: "If we love one another God lives in us, and his love is perfected in us. . . . There is no fear in love, but perfect love casts out fear" (1 Jn 4:12, 18).

Fear can be an overwhelming emotion; this may be a good thing if we are being chased by a bear in the woods. But when it is present in our marriage relationship it can be stifling, keeping us locked in the bond of our past. For better or for worse, we are all products of our past to some degree. Praise God, most of our past experiences are good and help us to become better people, better spouses. Even difficult experiences can be turned inside out through the love of our spouse.

Although I came back to the Church first and helped Teresa to find her way back, it is her deep love for Jesus in a very personal, down-to-earth way that has allowed me to grow spiritually and emotionally. To Teresa, Jesus is as real and present as you and me; but for me, Jesus tended to be more set apart. My relationship with God was more private, which isn't necessarily a bad thing, but one that I truly felt God calling me out of. I knew God wanted me to do more—to evangelize. But to be honest, I was afraid of failure. Teresa has helped my faith come alive by her witness, love, and support through those times when I was uncertain of God's desire for my life. I'm an introvert by nature, which for a long time was a quality I did not want or like, and it was something that at times bound my growth. Her constant encouragement, fearless example, and side-by-side support has had a huge impact on my faith life.

Saint John's encouragement that perfect love drives out fear is obviously referring to God's love being able to vanquish all fear, especially that of death and eternal separation from him. Our love may not be perfect, but Teresa's example of faith and her deep, sure love of me as she models Christ's acclimation to "be not afraid" has been of inestimable value in my faith journey and relationship growth with Jesus. So many times in scripture Jesus tells us, "Be not afraid," but I can truly say that would not have been possible for me without the love of my wife.

Tips to "Ransom the Captive"

Sometimes we can be our own worst enemies. We know God has forgiven us, but we can't forgive ourselves. Or maybe our partner still can't accept even God's forgiveness. What then? How can we begin to walk alongside our spouse, to "ransom the captive"?

Encourage your spouse with words of love and affirmation. Be generous in your praise, giving your spouse a fresh vision of the person you love, created by God for a unique and important purpose. Refuse to drag up past failures or berate him or her for current ones. Instead, "ransom" those areas where your spouse is held captive with your prayers and acts of heroic virtue. Notice what is good, honorable, and beautiful.

Remind your spouse of the healing power of the sacrament of Reconciliation. Recite these words to each other often: "Every saint has a past, every sinner has a future." Why not make it a once-a-month date to go to confession together—then get a treat!

Refuse to keep guilty secrets. Is there an area of your life where you are struggling to find freedom? Are you tempted to sneak that "guilty pleasure" when your spouse isn't looking to avoid a lecture or "the look"? Make a commitment to be accountable to one another and to pray for one another. Use it as an opportunity to grow in intimate grace!

Prayer of Release

Lord, you told us you came to set the captives free. Help us understand that our sins of the past, once confessed, are not only forgotten but also forgiven, and should never be a reason to keep us enslaved in shame and unworthiness and away from you. Amen.

Reflection Questions

1. What is one thing you most admire about your spouse? How do you wish you were more like him or her? What do you think he or she most struggles with? (Consider writing it down in a note to each other and allowing the other person to read it. Then discuss what you have learned.)

2. Is there an area of your life in which you still feel "captive" and in need of freedom? What is one way your spouse can help you, so you can be "ransomed" by the power of God's forgiveness?

3. In this chapter we explored how two apostles—Saint Peter and Judas—responded to personal failure. What do you think Jesus would say to you if you were to tell him about your "prison"? Why not tell him about it now?

4. How do you feel about going to confession? If you haven't gone in a long time, what is holding you back? Which is greater—the fear or your desire to receive the grace in store for you?

Seven

Bury the Dead

Respond to your spouse's deepest sorrows and regrets.

> Therefore we have been buried with him by baptism into death, so that, just as Christ was raised from the dead by the glory of the Father, so we too might walk in newness of life.
>
> *–Romans 6:4*

Teresa

I love the Serenity Prayer:

> God, grant me the serenity to accept the
> things I cannot change;
> courage to change the things I can;
> and wisdom to know the difference.

This short, twenty-five-word prayer packs a powerful punch and is a prayer that really makes a difference in our lives and relationships once we learn how to apply it effectively. When many of us read it, we get the sense that this is a really private prayer—something between only an individual and God to help someone deal with challenges and struggles and move beyond the pain or suffering of the past.

But what happens when we bring our spouse into the picture and find the courage to pray this prayer together? Amazing things can happen!

A few years ago, Dominick and I were vacationing in Italy, dining at one of our favorite ristorantes in Rome, when another American couple nearby asked us if we were just married. Apparently we were acting like newlyweds: holding hands, laughing, toasting with our wine glasses—just having way too much fun, I guess.

What a compliment! Dominick and I thanked them and chuckled to ourselves. "If they only knew our history," we said to each other, almost at the same time. It was indeed a compliment that our love for each other was so apparent even to strangers. And it's true—we are having more fun being with each other now than ever before, thanks be to God.

It wasn't always that way, of course. I deeply regretted all the time that was lost in the early years of our marriage: the Saturday nights, the holidays, the evenings spent arguing when we should have been spending time enjoying each other. I felt that we had not only hurt ourselves in those tumultuous times but God as well. He had given us this marriage as a gift to each other, and for too long we either took it for granted or, all too often, squandered it.

God, grant me the courage to accept the things I cannot change.

This short line challenges me and reminds me that there is indeed a time to "bury the dead," to let go of the regrets and sorrows of the past. None of us could ever be worthy of all the gifts God has given us and continues to give us. Saint John's gospel tells us "from his fullness we have all received, grace upon grace," or one blessing after another (Jn 1:16).

For several years, even after we had taken the first steps to heal our marriage, I kept waiting for, as the saying goes, the other shoe to drop. We didn't deserve to be happy, I told myself. We didn't deserve to be enjoying each other's company and feeling once again like lovesick newlyweds on their honeymoon.

Even today I sometimes find myself wondering why God is so incredibly good to us—not just to Teresa and Dominick but to every one of us. God is absolutely crazy head over heels in love with us, and there is nothing we can do to change that. It was my husband who helped me truly get a deeper understanding of the depths of God's love. My wondering is not focused on sadness or regret but instead on the awe of grasping what an incredibly merciful and loving Lord we serve.

The courage to change the things I can.

As we take the first steps to bury the regrets of the past, it's also important to learn from our mistakes and change the way we live. Dominick helped me apply the Romans

8:28 situation to our past: "We know that all things work together for good for those who love God, who are called according to his purpose."

I realized we had been given a second chance by God. Through our suffering we came to appreciate our marriage, especially our time together; even grocery shopping and household chores became more enjoyable, believe it or not. When you come close to losing everything, then everything—including the mundane responsibilities—becomes precious.

The wisdom to know the difference.

What's done is done. Unlike George Bailey in *It's a Wonderful Life* or Marty McFly in *Back to the Future*, we don't have our own time-traveling angel or magical DeLorean that can whisk us away to another time or place. The wisdom comes in knowing this fact, accepting it, grabbing the hand of your spouse, and moving forward.

Dominick

When I was growing up, one of my dad's favorite TV shows, in an odd sort of way, was the *Batman* series that aired in the early 1970s. He always got a kick out of how, no matter what peril Batman and Robin found themselves in—whether they were about to be dropped into a vat of bubbling acid or frozen alive in a giant ice cube—Batman always had just the right tool or gadget in his bat belt to save the day. My dad would always tease us as to how

Batman could have all those things in that one belt, but as kids we just thought it was great drama.

We will all face very difficult challenges in our lives; no one gets out of this world unscathed, whether by the actions of others, ourselves, or by the nature of life itself. Broken relationships, untimely deaths, poor decisions—all of these and many other events in our lives can be a source of sorrow or regret. Some we were probably helpless to do anything about; in others we may have been prominent players. Nonetheless, it can be very difficult to bring healing and closure to these difficult life circumstances.

Responding to your wife or husband who is struggling with such issues can be quite a challenge to both of you. Deep sorrows and regrets are not easily dismissed, nor should they be in most cases. One day they can be a distant memory; the next they can be in-your-face real. Wounds may have healed, but often the scars remain.

Many years ago, Teresa struggled with some poor decisions she had made years prior related to her demanding, high-profile career in the secular media. The consequences of these decisions had been more or less resolved, but the remorse lingered. Seeing her go through such pain and feeling ill-equipped to help her was stressful for our relationship.

Over time I realized that I needed to have a multi-faceted, Christ-like approach. In other words, sometimes Jesus wasn't interested in all the details and the nitty-gritty—he just offered compassion and forgiveness, as he did with the woman caught in adultery who was about to be stoned. Other times he was probing and challenging (as with the woman at the well). And sometimes he just gave and gave from the depths of his heart (such as when he fed the five thousand). There was never one approach, except that in love he always met people where they were and lifted them up by whatever means needed at the time, even if it meant turning over tables or driving out demons.

As a husband, my responsibility is to do the same wherever my wife is on any particular day. Much prayer is needed for insight and awareness of the many ways Satan stirs up sorrow and regret to derail relationships. Without being overly simplistic, it takes many forms of love.

I'm a big country music fan. One of my favorite artists is Martina McBride. One of my favorite songs of hers is about the trials and tribulations so many people contend with in everyday life and the response that others who are in a position to help have (or should have). It's the refrain of this song that always stirs my heart: "Love's the only house big enough for all the pain in the world."[1] This, coupled with "God is love" (1 Jn 4:8), greatly animates my role as a husband to help my wife put to rest her deepest sorrows and regrets. Love is the only house for all the pain in the world: love manifested in myriad ways, in whatever is needed at the time—just like Batman with his bat belt.

Tips to Help You Bury Regret

As Dominick pointed out in the preceding passage, Jesus used many approaches to meet the needs of people, especially those who were weighed down by life. When his friend Lazarus died, for example, he reacted in a most human fashion (in John 11:35 we read that "Jesus began to weep"). Then he worked a miracle by raising Lazarus from the dead. This combination of action and reaction is important when it comes to helping our partner to "bury the dead" and release the burden of regret. How do we begin?

Celebrate your life together as a married couple. Make the most of every day. Hold hands. Break out the good china. Create a scrapbook of your happiest moments.

Acknowledge the pain of the past, but do not allow yourself to "remain in the tomb." Pray for the grace to be like Lazarus: "Unbind him, and let him go" (Jn 11:44). Pray the Serenity Prayer together as you help each other let bygones be bygones.

Look to the future. Find some time every day, or at least several times a week, to talk about your hopes and dreams. Pray together often, as a couple, for the grace to "run with endurance," side by side, in the race of life. Be sure to thank God for those in heaven who are praying for you as you run!

68   Intimate Graces

Prayer of Buried Regret

God, grant us the serenity to accept the things we
cannot change; courage to change the things we
can; and wisdom to know the difference. In all
these things, help us to experience your love and
mercy, so that we may know new life as husband
and wife. Amen.

Reflection Questions

1. Is there something in your past, perhaps even something you have already shared with your spouse, that
is still affecting your marriage today?

2. Why do you think you or your spouse is unable to
bury the regrets of the past?

3. How do you think your spouse could help you move
past these issues and "bury the dead"?

4. Have you brought this issue to confession, so that you
might receive strength from the Lord to release the burden you are carrying? Consider making arrangements
to receive the sacrament of Reconciliation this week.

Eight

Instruct the Ignorant

*Embrace marriage as an ongoing
path to discovery.*

⸻

[God our savior] desires everyone to be saved
and to come to the knowledge of the truth.

—1 Timothy 2:4

Teresa

Perhaps no area of marriage is more of a minefield for couples than the issue of money: who makes it, who saves it, and who spends it. Learning to work together as a couple to make sound financial decisions can be difficult.

Our friends Thomas and Maria Herbel have quite a story to tell regarding money and marriage. We met the Herbels on our first marriage cruise cohosted by Dominick and me along with Greg and Julie Alexander of the Alexander House. Part of our cruise experience was to allow the couples participating to share their thoughts and concerns during my live radio broadcast.

As Tom and Maria explained, they were both ignorant when it came to money management. After hitting rock bottom, they knew they had to instruct each other by holding each other accountable. They soon learned that their efforts would have positive effects on a lot more than just their bank accounts.

The Herbels learned the hard way that having your financial house in order is an important step in building a healthy, lifelong marriage. "Oh, my gosh, we were in debt up to our eyeballs!" Maria remembers. "But . . . how could this be? How could we be in so much debt if we both had well-paying jobs? We fought and fought over bills, and each of us had our own priorities about spending. We were definitely not on the same page, financially speaking; our spending was out of control, and it was ruining our marriage."

Revolving credit led to consumer debt in excess of $120,000 (not counting the mortgage), with ten active credit cards, several with balances exceeding $20,000. They used credit cards to finance vacations, car repairs, Catholic school tuition, medical bills, home repairs . . . and on and on, usually paying the minimum balance due. "It was *financial suicide*," they both agreed.

Around that time, they heard of a Christian financial planner who had a system to help people out of debt, and they attended the classes and bought the books. In the process, they discovered that they had a spending problem and needed a written budget. "This program was an answer to prayer," they both said. Together they learned to manage their money, and they worked together to achieve financial freedom.

"We asked for each other's forgiveness and asked God for forgiveness too," Maria said. Tom agreed. "We established a budget and vowed to keep each other accountable. We stopped eating out, didn't go on vacations, dropped cable TV, and said no to nonessential spending. And you know what happened? We had fewer arguments . . . even our children noticed we weren't fighting as much!"

Five years later, they continue to live on a written budget. Their credit cards are paid off, they have money in savings, have paid off student loans, and pay for vacations in cash. "We are building our retirement accounts and are teaching our children to live within their means and save for the future," Thomas said.

The Herbels just celebrated their thirtieth anniversary on a marriage cruise with Dom and me and the Alexanders. "We paid for it in cash before we got on the ship!" the Herbels told us. "It was a sweet moment in our marriage, a time to celebrate and reward each other for instituting discipline in our finances. And it was a time to get away to enjoy each other's company and commit to making our marriage even better!"

Dominick

First Plato gave us: "Know thyself." This gives us a useful bit of direction.

Benjamin Franklin said it a bit differently: "Three things are hard: steel, diamonds, and to know thyself." This, too, is a bit of useful wit.

However, it was Saint John Paul II who said it best of all, unlocking the mystery of love with beautiful, simple language: "Only in Christ can men and women find answers to the ultimate questions that trouble them. Only in Christ can they fully understand their dignity as persons created and loved by God."[1]

This last quote reveals a wonderful insight into one of man's deepest desires: to know God and to know who we are. To know ourselves we must "lose ourselves in Jesus" and, because we are prideful human beings who tend to be somewhat blind to the real truth about the person in the mirror, God gave us the perfect reminder in marriage.

Next to Jesus, there is no one who knows me better than my wife; yes, even better than I know myself (or will at least admit to myself). As my partner for "the whole of life" (*Catechism*, 1601), Teresa knows my hopes and dreams, fears and disappointments, and, most importantly, what I want to be when I grow up. I say that "what I want to be when I grow up" a little bit tongue-in-cheek but also with much seriousness. When we were growing up—maybe in grade school or junior high—we were all probably asked that question many times. We tend to think of the answer as something static, such as a fireman or policeman. For me, I wanted to be a helicopter pilot. (I don't remember why, I just thought it was cool; even today I would still like to ride in one just once.) However, our lives aren't static, and our relationships with one another and with God certainly aren't, either.

Through my marriage I've been able to grow, learn, experience, and discover things that I never would have without Teresa. And that's different than saying "without a wife." Because God is the author of our marriages, we are together for a reason and a purpose. We are on this journey together, and as much as I would like a clear, straight path, we can barely see around the next bend in the road. Every day is a new experience, but we experience it together with the Lord at our side.

Let's face it: life is one new experience after another; or, as the saying goes, "Life is what happens while you're making plans." As Jesus emptied himself on the cross so that we might have life to the fullest, the same is true in marriage—when I give all that I am to my wife and she does the same, each more concerned with the other, the world opens wide to experience God and creation in all its beauty. There is such freedom in the mutual love and trust of husband and wife; with this freedom comes growth and discovery in our humanity, spirituality, and our relationship with God and each other. Each day is not to be feared but to be lived.

There was a period in my life when I went through great anxiety about my career, my health, God's call in my life, and so on. It was a time of second-guessing and doubt. Through the entire time I knew of Teresa's full love and support regardless. I learned a lot about myself and my relationship with the Lord, and obviously much about Teresa's love for me, because it gave me the freedom and courage to learn. As Jesus broke the yoke of death for us and allowed us to grow in our love and knowledge of him, so does a marriage when we give to the other more than we are in turn willing to receive.

Tips for Enlightening with Love

Are you indulging in some habit or other behavior that you both know is unhealthy for your marriage and family life? While nagging and shaming are usually counterproductive, there are some ways you can encourage the one you love to get back on track.

Be patient and pray for a change of heart. Oftentimes in marriage, one partner may be miles ahead on the path to discovery. If you're the one in the faith "fast lane," give your spouse a chance to catch up.

Model gentleness and compassion. Think about some regular opportunities to help each other grow. Talk about what you gained from the Sunday homily. Invite your spouse to attend a Catholic conference or to listen to a Catholic speaker in your area and make it a date night.

Tend to your own garden. Be careful not to deflect the work God is trying to do in *you* by focusing too much on your spouse's faults. Feed yourself spiritually while walking along the journey of discovery with your spouse. If your spouse is engaged in unhealthy, addictive behavior, seek professional help and guidance for both of you.

Prayer for Wisdom

Lord, help us discover more about you as we discover more about ourselves. Help us to be open to loving instruction. Give us the grace to admit and address serious issues that may be causing problems in our relationship. Amen.

Reflection Questions

1. How have you helped or instructed each other in the important areas of your life together? How have you helped each other grow in your relationship with God and the Church?

2. What have you learned (or do you think you can learn to appreciate) from each other in terms of your spouse's gifts and talents?

3. Do either or both of you have difficulty receiving loving admonishment from the other? If so, why? What might each of you do to improve?

Nine

Counsel the Doubtful

See marriage as a faith-builder.

The first duty of love is to listen.

—Paul Tillich

Teresa

Although marriage counselors and other therapists use a variety of methods and approaches to help their clients, most counseling sessions do have one common denominator: the client or patient, not the counselor, does most of the talking. The counselor poses questions, but for the most part he or she simply listens and allows the clients to express themselves.

Unfortunately, many spouses (including myself) sometimes assume that if we only say just the right words, or if our partner would only listen to the wisdom we have to offer, the other person would surely have his own epiphany or "come to Jesus" moment and the two of you would see the world through the same faith-colored glasses.

Oh, if only real life worked that way.

My husband has always had a gift for reaching even those furthest from God, as I once was. His style is quite different from mine for, as you may have read, we are total opposites. But his peaceful, reflective demeanor and the deep, thoughtful way he teaches about Christ and the Church have a profound impact on many people. Our dear friends Lynn and Don Bernard from Ohio would be the first to testify to Dom's positive influence.

We met Lynn and Don on a Caribbean cruise twenty-two years ago while we were both celebrating our tenth anniversaries. We hit it off right away and were inseparable for the rest of the trip, and we have been very good friends ever since. Because Dayton and Detroit are only a few hours apart, we manage to see each other at least once a year. Lynn and Don are both strong Christians who attend a nondenominational church. They have been very respectful of our faith, and sincerely interested in what we practice and why.

One evening, after yet another fun-filled weekend together, Lynn asked Dom some poignant questions that both encouraged and frightened him. She told him how much she enjoyed listening to him explain Catholic teaching and how he was one of the few people who really seemed to able to explain it in a way anyone in or outside the Church could understand. "As a married man in the Church, what can *you* do? How can *you* serve?" she asked.

"Although I can't be a priest, there is a lot I can do," Dom replied. "I can be a lay minister—you know, maybe teaching or leading a ministry at the parish or diocesan level. I can also become a deacon. But there is an awful lot of studying involved in becoming a deacon. And I don't think I have the right personality for the diaconate. Most deacons I know are real extroverts."

"You really need to pray about becoming a deacon," Lynn said. "You certainly have a gift for reaching people. Again, pray about it."

Lynn was one of the first in our circle to suggest my husband consider the diaconate. Several others—some close to us, some mere acquaintances—would eventually do the same on their own, seemingly out of the blue. Independently, they were confirming my own heartfelt thoughts regarding Dom's diaconate discernment. Deep down I believed if Dom could be a major instrument in getting someone like me back to the faith then, for crying out loud, he was practically a miracle worker and could help anyone!

Because of Lynn and others like her who encouraged my husband to take this next step, I found myself becoming more vocal in my own encouragement of him. After all, I truly saw him as a deacon. And these additional "attaboys" were all I needed to continually remind my husband of why I believed he was deacon material.

Of course, it wasn't my decision. It had to be his. While the wife plays a crucial role in diaconate formation and must be in full support of her husband's choice, he has to discern and decide if he has a call to serve God in this very unique and powerful way. This is not an easy process for anyone. It is even more challenging for someone like my husband—an engineer who by his own admission struggles with "analysis paralysis." I did my best to cheer him on, reminding him of all he had done for me. But sometimes when it comes from someone so close to you, it's not very convincing.

"Of course you support me," Dom observed. "You're supposed to support me. That's what wives do." I took these words to heart and challenged myself to find better ways to apply this particular spiritual work of mercy. For example, I learned to listen more closely to Dom's fears and concerns and to ask questions. Dom had to learn not only to accept the areas in his spirituality that were lacking but also to accept the positive feedback regarding his many spiritual gifts. God was using this "counseling the doubtful" to build up our marriage and each other as well. Go figure.

Dominick

One of the adjectives that would quickly come to mind in describing my wife, even for someone who just met her, would be *fearless*. As a street reporter for more than twenty years, she was never afraid to ask the tough questions or cover the difficult stories. If you read a few chapters in this book, you have probably already become familiar with her passion for justice and protecting the defenseless. I have never seen Teresa shrink away from doing the right thing or at least trying to do it amidst opposing forces that were very often out of her control, especially when she was a secular news reporter.

So you would never think a person like Teresa would have self-doubts or anxieties. That's what I thought for a long time too. How could someone who does what I could never do in a million years have self-doubt about other areas of her life that seem so easy or trivial to me? I didn't feel comfortable pushing her about these things, though. I think it was partly because I have such confidence and admiration for her character, and partly because of my own selfish reluctance not to get too much into the nitty-gritty of things or to risk an unpleasant reaction from her.

Over time, God began to show me one particular area of growth for both of us: accepting God's forgiveness and forgiving ourselves when we failed each other. There was a very difficult stretch in our marriage when we were having trouble and needed to forgive each other for the hurts we had inflicted upon one another. But Teresa was really struggling with accepting God's forgiveness and with self-forgiveness. She was sure that receiving God's forgiveness through the sacrament of Reconciliation couldn't be that easy—and that forgiving herself was even harder! God's mercy was having a difficult time penetrating her heart.

This was frustrating for me, because I knew we *both* knew the facts: Jesus died for our sins, and through the sacrament of the Church his grace is abundantly available to us. Even so, Teresa doubted that she could be truly and fully forgiven. I had no doubt that God was waiting to do just that! As an engineer, I found it difficult to understand how we could both look at the facts and arrive at such very different conclusions. What I never stopped to consider was the fact that my wife has always worn her heart on her sleeve. What she needed was not a catechetical discussion but a *pastoral* one.

Sometimes it can be difficult to minister effectively to those closest to us. Maybe it's because we know too much, in a sense. It can be so much easier to be patient and tender with strangers. With a spouse, we know what she is capable of, what she has experienced in the past, and how her faith has grounded her in other areas of her life. We lose sight of the fact that everyone has times of weakness and doubt. All of us need to be reminded—patiently and gently—of the truth of God's love and care.

I had to learn to be patient yet persistent in helping Teresa to see God's love for her and for us in other aspects of our life. I tried to help her nibble away at the doubt she was carrying, to provide times of respite to mentally, spiritually, or physically get away from the issue for a while. Ultimately, though, my role was to help Teresa restore her trust in the power of God to "make all things new" (Rev 21:5).

We all have some doubt at times regarding the power of God in our lives. The opening scene of *The Passion of the Christ* shows the devil whispering doubts into Jesus' ear as he agonizes in the garden. We know the doubts are not true, but they can linger and eventually take root in a big way. My role as a husband is to help my wife rise above the wave of doubt and have the courage to stomp on its head in the way that best fits her.

Tips for Affirming Your Partner in Times of Doubt

Whether you are experiencing self-doubt or a crisis of faith—or are noticing these things in your partner—these moments often present unique opportunities to give and experience intimate grace within your marriage. What are some gentle ways to practice this spiritual work of mercy in order to draw the two of you closer together?

Help the doubtful one regain perspective. Build some quality and quiet time together into your weekly routine. Let this be a chance for you to listen to each other and take a sincere interest in what might be on your spouse's heart.

Offer to pray with your doubting spouse, and together ask the Lord for wisdom and insight. Encourage each other to grow in your personal relationship with Jesus, but understand that God's timing is different for each of us. Pray for each other and use this particular spiritual work of mercy as another chance for you to grow in holiness.

Give each other space. If your partner is wrestling with doubts, God may choose to use another person or some other source of wisdom to speak to your spouse's heart. At times like this, extending "intimate grace" to your spouse may mean stepping back and praying for God to bring the right person or timely message when your spouse is ready to listen. Pray for the grace to "wait upon the Lord" with patience, expecting him to work.

Prayer to Build Up Faith

Lord, show us how to be more like you and to really learn to listen to those we love. When I am doubtful, help me to trust you to bring clarity and wisdom. Amen.

Reflection Questions

1. Outside of weekly church attendance, how often do you and your spouse do faith-based activities together? What kinds of activities do you think you would enjoy?

2. Pope Francis continues to remind Catholics and all Christians to read the scriptures. Are you and your spouse reading God's Word daily? How might you strengthen your faith as a couple by sharing what you are discovering in God's Word?

3. Do either of you struggle with some aspect of the faith or a particular teaching? What, if anything, are you doing to overcome this hurdle? Are you willing to relinquish your doubts and seek the truth, or at least pray for the grace to be willing to do so? Consider making an appointment with your pastor or a spiritual director if you would like to resolve this issue but don't know where to begin.

Ten

Admonish the Sinner

*Strengthen your marriage by breaking the
influence of serious (grave) sin.*

‖‖‖

Let the word of Christ dwell in you richly;
teach and admonish one another in all wisdom;
and with gratitude in your hearts sing psalms,
hymns, and spiritual songs to God.

—Colossians 3:16

Teresa

When God created marriage, he designed sexual intimacy
to be a beautiful reflection of self-giving, lifelong love. It
is no wonder, then, that the enemy works so hard to twist
and distort the beauty of married love . . . or that porn
addiction is at epidemic proportions, with the porn indus-
try earning ninety-seven billion dollars a year worldwide.
While most of us instinctively recoil at violent or depraved
expressions of human sexuality, such as child pornography or domestic violence, the gradual dulling of cultural

sensibilities has resulted in a growing acceptance of things that not long ago would have been equally unthinkable.

To take just one example, a few years ago during a discussion on my daily radio program concerning the spread of pornography, we had a surprising caller. It wasn't a wife calling up to express concern about her husband's pornography addiction. In this case, the wife had the issue, and her husband wasn't quite sure what to make of it.

This was shortly after the blockbuster "mommy porn" series Fifty Shades hit the bookstore shelves. (The film version was released on Valentine's Day weekend 2015.) The caller wasn't quite sure what to make of his wife's choice of reading material; according to him, his wife just saw the books as a form of entertainment. But the husband had heard his friends talking about the series—many of their wives were also reading it—and so when he came home one day and noticed *Fifty Shades of Grey* on the nightstand, he began browsing through it.

He was stunned and confused at the graphic nature of what he read. Based on an abusive, sadomasochistic relationship between a successful businessman and a shy college graduate, the Fifty Shades trilogy is harmful because it "normalizes and glamorizes" intimate partner violence, according to a study published in the *Journal of Women's Health*.[1] In the first book, young college student Anastasia Steele is stalked, isolated, threatened, physically bound, and then whipped during sexual encounters with the smooth business tycoon Christian Grey. The series chronicles the relationship, adding to a growing body of literature "noting dangerous violence standards being perpetuated in popular culture," according to the study.

Why would any woman find these books attractive or exciting to read about, the caller wondered? What did his wife's attraction to these books say not only about her but about their relationship? Did this mean that she would eventually start asking or wanting her husband to dominate her in the bedroom? He couldn't imagine a man treating a woman so horribly. He was truly bewildered by it all and was wondering what, if anything, he should say to his wife.

Live talk radio obviously doesn't make for an ideal setting for Christian counseling. It's not meant to be. But responsible hosts and their guests do try to offer guidelines and some general advice from solid sources. The Catholic psychologist on the air with me that day agreed that this was definitely something this concerned husband needed to address with his wife. *Fifty Shades of Grey* is pornographic. Just because it comes in the form of a fictional book or film does not make it okay. The Church teaches that pornography is a grave offense. It's not a matter of opinion or personal taste but a grave sin, as we read in the *Catechism*:

> Pornography consists in removing real or simulated sexual acts from the intimacy of the partners in order to display them deliberately to third parties. It offends against

> chastity because it perverts the conjugal act,
> the intimate giving of spouses to each other.
> It does grave injury to the dignity of its par-
> ticipants (actors, vendors, the public), since
> each one becomes an object of base pleasure
> and illicit profit for others. It immerses all
> who are involved in the illusion of a fantasy
> world. It is a grave offense. Civil authorities
> should prevent the production and distribu-
> tion of pornographic materials. (CCC 2354)

What, then, was this husband to do?

Marriage is an ongoing path to discovery—discovery about each other and discovery about God and his Church. If marriage is a sacrament ordered to the good of the other person, and if a spouse is charged with helping his partner get to heaven, then part of that "discovery" is going to involve the kind of frank and honest discussion that may at times be uncomfortable, given the toxic culture that exists today.

Jesus came to comfort the afflicted and afflict the comfortable. If we want a truly intimate marriage that is touched by God's grace, it will mean moving out of our comfort zones. At times we may even be called to lovingly instruct our spouse along the path regarding an area of Church teaching that stands in stark contrast to what the world has long accepted or normalized.

We can't force our spouses to accept the teachings of the Church, but we are called to be faithful—both to our spouses and to the Lord—nevertheless. As we prayerfully and lovingly continue to encourage those we love to come to a full understanding of *why* the Church teaches what it teaches, I know from personal experience that this can prove to be a tremendous source of intimate grace.

I remember digging in my heels on a number of Church teachings after Dominick came back to the faith. I still considered myself Catholic even though I knew very little about what my faith actually taught. I had just swallowed the cultural definitions. It was a combination of Dominick's witness and my own rocky journey of discovery that eventually brought me around. Dominick lovingly challenged me, prayed for me practically 24/7, and over time learned how to witness in a variety of ways.

To this day I wonder what happened to that dear man who called in to my program years ago. I never heard from him again. He never did share just how much he actually knew about Church teaching, but he knew enough to sense something was wrong. I hope and pray he was able to lovingly challenge his wife, and that they continued to grow in their understanding of authentic love and truth, for the sake of their marriage . . . and for the sake of their souls.

Dominick

"There is no such thing as a private sin." I don't know where I first heard that or even if I believed it when I did, but I have come to understand the profound truth in it. No matter how isolated or self-absorbed the sin might be, it has an effect on many others in our life. It is not different in many ways than a virus that we might unwittingly transmit to someone else—they then do the same, but the source was our sin, not necessarily theirs.

Pornography or abortion or illicit sex are a few of the sins that come to mind that are often received or understood as a "personal choice." The pressure to "go along to get along" has probably been around since Adam and Eve. But it seems so much more pervasive today, with more devastating consequences. The grip of those kinds of sin—or any sin for that matter—can be especially difficult to break. The best approach is to speak the truth in love, not condemning the sinner but rather the sin. So often I hear people complain that the Church has "all of these rules and regulations," with the implication that our free will is being suppressed. However, our will is not free when it is held captive by sin and restrained from knowing the love of God and others in our lives.

Not long ago I preached a homily on the sacredness of marriage between a man and a woman as God's plan of creation. After Mass a woman approached me asking me if I really believed in what I had said during the homily. I sensed we were not on the same page. I explained that not only did I believe it, but marriage between one man and one woman is what the Church teaches emphatically. I tried to nicely explain a little bit more about the fact that God's plan for the fulfillment of man and woman is found in God and each other, and that the Church teaches what she does for our own good, not to limit or suffocate us.

Although this parishioner was not combative, she was also not interested in hearing what I was trying to say. She walked away after politely telling me she would not be returning to our parish. I truly felt compassion for her; she was stirred to talk but not stirred enough to consider what I was trying to say. I thought of the rich young man who wouldn't and couldn't follow Jesus when the Lord asked him to sell everything and follow him (see Mk 10:17–31).

In our marriage, Teresa and I try to be as open as we can toward each other when one sees something that is not right or if one needs to talk about a perplexing dilemma. We try our best not to be judgmental; we try to evaluate subjective personal motives while sticking to the objective issue. We do this because of our love for each other and desire for the other to be the best he or she can be before God's glory and as a good witness to others. We have to be careful not to let this dissolve into nagging or being overly scrupulous, but most of the time these situations will lead to meaningful discussions about ourselves, God, and his role in our life, which far exceeds in value what prompted the initial discussion.

We have found speaking the truth in love and helping to carry each other's burdens to be a wonderful, uplifting part of our marriage.

Tips for Admonishing a Loved One Caught in Sin

When we make choices that are against Catholic moral teaching, it damages both our relationships with other people and, even more importantly, our relationship with God. And since the goal of marriage is to help each other to heaven, authentic intimacy requires that we be ready to speak the truth, lovingly and clearly, rather than turn a blind eye in order to achieve a false peace. If you noticed an ugly mole growing on your loved one's back, you would insist that your partner see the doctor! In the same way, serious sin requires the attention of the Great Physician within the healing sacrament of confession.

So, where do you start? Here are some tips to keep in mind.

Make sure your own conscience is clear and that you have prayerfully considered your spouse's point of view. If you are constantly nagging or fault-finding with your spouse, you may find that it is difficult to get the desired response when you really do need him or her to listen. If you want

God to change your spouse, ask him to begin with you! Be careful to behave in ways that are consistent with the truth, even if your spouse does not. At the same time affirm, build up, and be generous in your admiration when your spouse makes good choices. And don't forget to admit when *you* have been in the wrong.

Consider whether the behavior constitutes serious sin or is simply an annoying habit. The Church's definition of mortal sin is found in the *Catechism*: "For a sin to be mortal, three conditions must together be met: 'Mortal sin is sin whose object is grave matter and which is also committed with full knowledge and deliberate consent'" (CCC 1857). "Admonishing the sinner," then, means helping each other to discern whether a particular behavior meets these criteria or is hurting your relationships with each other or with God.

If your spouse's behavior is endangering you or other family members physically, emotionally, or spiritually, consider talking to your pastor or other spiritually mature counselor. In Matthew 18:15–20, we find that there is a time to "shine a light" on spiritual sickness. Within marriage, helping a spouse to heaven sometimes means being there to help our partner get up after he or she has fallen by the side of the path. However, if your spouse is determined to march over a cliff, you are not obligated to endanger yourself! Seeking wise spiritual counsel will help you discern the right thing to do.

Prayer for a Clean Heart

Dear God, we know that we have all sinned and
fall short of your glory. In your mercy and kindness we ask for the grace and humility to help each
other see the way we should follow, the truth we
should know, and the life that you offer us through
your son, Jesus Christ. Amen.

Reflection Questions

1. Do you or your spouse have any grave or mortal sins
   you are dealing with currently or in the past that need
   to be confessed—to God and to each other?

2. Is your marriage being affected by culturally accept-
   able but sinful habits? Consider what culturally accept-
   able but potentially damaging practices one or both of
   you need to relinquish: the excessive consumption of
   food or alcohol, gambling, overuse of technology, or
   perhaps even excessive work habits. Have you considered talking to a priest and/or a counselor about the
   sin or sins affecting your marriage and your relationship with God?

3. Are there areas of the Church's dogmatic teaching
    (such as the teachings on sexuality and contracep-
    tion) that you and your spouse have rejected or are
    still seeking to understand?

4. What can you do to be more open to understanding,
    accepting, and practicing the teachings of the Church?
    If you sense that God is asking you to discuss this with
    your spouse, have you asked for both the strength and
    the opportunity?

Eleven

Bear Wrongs Patiently

The benefits of forbearance in marriage.

Many marriages would be better if the husband
and the wife clearly understood that they are on
the same side.

–Zig Ziglar

Bear one another's burdens . . .

–Galatians 6:2

Teresa

When we met Otto and Erika Soeding on our marriage
cruise, we were struck by their unique stories of weath-
ering marital storms related to their faith traditions. In
some ways, their journey is similar to ours, as even though
they were both Christians, one spouse was on the faith
fast track and the other was still contemplating buying
that train ticket, so to speak. They would learn, as we did,
that allowing the spouse to travel at his or her own pace

would eventually lead to a more meaningful faith journey together.

Their journey of loving faith illustrates in a unique way how two very different people, being pulled by outside influences, can experience truly intimate grace by being patient and loving, willing to make personal sacrifices out of love rather than each insisting "my way or the highway."

Otto and Erika met more than fifty years ago, on July 1, 1961. On Christmas 1962, they promised to spend the rest of their lives together—despite the fact that Otto was Catholic and Erika was Lutheran. "It was a very emotional time for us," Otto remembers. "We almost broke up!"

Erika left a well-paying job and moved to Switzerland to get the space she needed to come to terms with her family's disapproval of Otto because of his faith. Neither of their families was especially devout. Erika's parents didn't go to church (she went with her grandmother); Otto's father had died when he was just eight years old, and his family didn't talk very much about Church teaching. So, to make things easier, Otto agreed to be married in the Lutheran church, as Erika was not ready to become Catholic, and they were married on May 28, 1965. They had their first child in March 1967, and shortly thereafter the couple moved to the United States, where they have lived for the past forty-seven years.

"Otto was unable to receive Communion as a Catholic because he got married in the Lutheran church, and

I could see he was suffering," Ericka recalls. "Finally, in 1971, Father Prus married us in the Shrine of the Little Flower in Royal Oak, Michigan. Otto was working for General Motors. He loved his family and his job and had several assignments overseas."

Time passed, and the Holy Spirit continued to work in their hearts, slowly. In 2004, when the movie *The Passion of the Christ* came out, Otto was deeply touched by the experience of watching it. He went to confession and in the evenings began watching EWTN. When they bought a winter home in Sarasota, Florida, they attended a pig roast hosted by the local Knights of Columbus; Otto became a fourth-degree Knight.

Erika also found herself drawn to Otto's faith, and when her parents died she enrolled in the RCIA program and was confirmed at the Easter Vigil in 2008 at the Shrine of the Little Flower. Together they serve as eucharistic ministers. "EWTN and Ave Maria Radio have both contributed to where we are today," Otto says. "Their wonderful programs helped us on our journey."

In Otto and Erika's story we see a beautiful image of what it means to practice the virtue of forbearance, the spiritual work of mercy to "bear wrongs patiently." This is an act that goes far beyond not losing your temper over everyday annoyances or willingly and quickly accepting an apology. Within marriage, this spiritual work of mercy must be applied in a much broader context. Patience does come to mind and is a part of forbearance, of course; when looking at the big picture of what it means between a husband and wife, one can see *why* it is so very important.

Otto was forbearing when he didn't insist that Erika override her own misgivings as well as her family's objections in order to get married in the Catholic Church. He might have insisted that his wife become Catholic so their children might be baptized in the faith; instead, he followed the prompting of the Holy Spirit and trusted in God's time.

In this way, Otto imitated the self-sacrificing love of Christ, who "does not deal with us according to our sins, nor repay us according to our iniquities" (Ps 103:10). Erika, for her part, saw just how much Otto loved her and was willing to give up for her. In time, his patient forbearance drew her to reconsider her initial resistance to the Catholic faith. He had extended truly intimate grace to his wife, loving her to the point that he refused his "rights" as husband and father, sensing that God was leading him to respond in a different way.

What was it that made Otto show such patience and forbearance with his wife? The answer might be found in Saint Matthew's Gospel (18:21–35) in the parable of the ungrateful servant. The master showed great compassion to the servant who owed him so much, forgiving him not just part of the amount he owed but the entire debt.

In the original parable, the servant did not fully accept that his debt had been paid but scurried about trying to raise the money by force:

But that same slave, as he went out, came upon one of his fellow slaves who owed him a hundred denarii; and seizing him by the throat, he said, "Pay what you owe." Then his fellow slave fell down and pleaded with him, "Have patience with me, and I will pay you." But he refused; then he went and threw him into prison until he should pay the debt. When his fellow slaves saw what had happened, they were greatly distressed, and they went and reported to their lord all that had taken place. Then his lord summoned him and said to him, "You wicked slave! I forgave you all that debt because you pleaded with me. Should you not have had mercy on your fellow slave, as I had mercy on you?" And in anger his lord handed him over to be tortured until he should pay his entire debt. (Mt 18:28–34)

In the story of Otto and Erika, we see a couple who gave love and grew in faith freely, not out of a sense of obligation or debt, but in a way that imitated the love of Christ: with forgiveness, empathy, and compassion—taking on himself a debt we could never pay ourselves. Through the sacrament of marriage, we have a unique opportunity to "pay it forward," letting our spouse grow in his or her own time, trusting the Holy Spirit to move in his or her life on his own timetable, rather than demanding our "rights."

How often do we need to practice this lesson of forbearance? This, too, we learn from the parable of the unforgiving servant:

> Then Peter came to Jesus and asked, "Lord, how many times shall I forgive my brother or sister who sins against me? Up to seven times?" Jesus answered, "I tell you, not seven times, but seventy-seven times." (Mt 18:22)

In what area of your marriage is the Holy Spirit giving you the opportunity to practice forbearance today?

Dominick

We've all heard the expression, "He has the patience of Job." Well, that's not exactly me—or at least it hasn't been for a good part of my life, including my married life. For the longest time I had a very short fuse, especially with inanimate objects: Christmas-tree lights that would work before you put them on the tree but then not after; nuts and bolts that wouldn't line up when assembling things; Tab A that would not fit into Slot B no matter how hard you hit it with a hammer. It didn't take much to get me irritated way beyond anything close to normal. But it wasn't just with tabs and slots; it was with people, too—especially my wife. I was part back-seat driver, part Monday-morning quarterback, and almost always "my way or the wrong way." And usually it was silly, stupid stuff and not the big important stuff that was at issue. I say this not to partially excuse myself but just the opposite—the everyday stuff made the everyday not so harmonious at home.

We laugh about these things now, but there was a time when my behavior was a real source of discontent in our marriage. Teresa felt like no matter what she did or how she did it, I would criticize. I thought she was too sensitive and that I was only trying to help her do it better, faster, whatever. What developed was a very tit-for-tat relationship that sucked the life out of our marriage in a most insidious way.

"All have sinned and fall short of the glory of God" (Rom 3:23). As with most "aha" scripture moments in my life, this verse hit me like a ton of bricks one day. I had read it before and internally nodded my head in understanding of the human condition, but this time it jumped off the page as a personal indictment of how I wasn't living my life in gratitude to God and my attitude toward others in my life, especially my wife. I understood this now with my heart as well as my head. God's patient mercy trumps all my sinful ways, especially the little everyday indiscretions that only he and I know about.

The ramifications of this verse began to seep through my whole life in understanding not only the virtue of patience but also forbearance: the necessity of refraining from doing or saying something I truly had a right to say or do. In marriage, it is not about turning a blind eye to sin so much as turning the other cheek over small annoyances and inconveniences, about coming to know the joy and freedom of living the partnership for the whole of life that God intends in a marriage.

With freedom comes great responsibility; at times I have a responsibility to act, as we read in Ephesians 4:15, "speaking the truth in love." At other times I have a responsibility not to do anything—to bear a wrong patiently and to "take one for the team." Our marriage is so much more diverse, so much more fun, and richer in so many ways because we have each other's back, knowing that in the other person there is great trust and support; there is no fear or anxiety.

Bearing wrongs patiently doesn't mean I am a doormat. Instead, it's more like a welcome mat for my wife to know of my love and God's love for her. Life can be difficult. We all make mistakes, and forbearance gives the opportunity to bear a burden for the sake of another as Jesus did for each of us, for all have sinned and all fall short of the glory of God.

Tips to Help You Forbear in Love

Marriages are like snowflakes: no two are exactly alike, and each of them looks dramatically different when viewed up close! The personalities, needs, and fears of each partner require a unique kind of intimate grace from his or her spouse. Here are some practical suggestions to help you better give and receive that kind of customized forbearance in your own marriage.

Sit down together and read Matthew 18:21–35. Think about some specific examples of how your spouse over the years has been more like the forgiving master than the ungrateful servant—even though you may have deserved much worse. Share those examples with each other, thanking each other for the gift of forbearance in your relationship.

Is there a particular area of your marriage you feel the need to "pull away" or hide because you are afraid you will be criticized or rejected? Consider making an appointment with your pastor or counselor to help you acquire some new communication skills. Or consider putting your feelings in a letter or journal, and let him or her reciprocate in writing. Sometimes, communicating in writing can take the pressure off!

Consider how the values and beliefs of your own family of origin are enhancing or straining your marriage. For example, if your family had dinner together every night, and your husband must work several evenings a week, could this be an opportunity for forbearance? If your mother made all her own clothes, and your spouse is a "fashionista" who loves to shop, what does forbearance look like in your situation?

Prayer of Patient Forbearance

Lord, slow us down. When we are ready to once again pounce on our partner, remind us that we are all sinners and all fall short. Give us the grace to remember that the only way we are going to help each other get to heaven is to be more like you. Amen.

Reflection Questions

1. How has your spouse's willingness or forbearance made a difference in your relationship?

2. How has your spouse's forbearance helped you grow closer not only to each other but also to God?

3. What advice would you give to another couple regarding the importance of forbearance in marriage?

Twelve

Forgive Offenses Willingly

*Experience the merciful balm of
forgiveness in marriage.*

To be a Christian means to forgive the inexcusable
because God has forgiven the inexcusable in you.

–C. S. Lewis

Teresa

Do you want to feel a lot more like that couple dancing on
the beach in the Sandals Resort commercial and a lot less
like the argumentative comic-strip couple Leroy and Loretta
Lockhorn? Speaking from a lot of experience, when you're
in the midst of rough spots in your relationship, you may
think having a more peaceful, loving, and less-stressful exis-
tence with your spouse is about as far away as an island in
the Caribbean. But it's actually a lot closer than you might
think. It's found in the balm of forgiveness, a balm that
can not only heal relationships but also affect how we feel
physically.

Some friends of ours, Dawn and Jamie, recently shared with us their story and told us of a series of choices—including premarital sex, contraception, and infidelity—that had long-lasting effects on their marriage. After their first child was diagnosed with autism, and the second eight weeks premature, Jamie had a vasectomy to eliminate the possibility of having more children.

"We were active members in our parish, regularly attending Mass, leading youth group, and serving the poor," said Jamie. "We did not see or feel the effects of our poor decision right away, but then the devil, in his cunning and devious fashion, had planted the seeds of deception and disillusionment that grew over time."

Six months after his operation, Jamie had an extramarital affair. Dawn recalled that the five months that followed her discovery of his affair were "volatile, and the outlook of our marriage was very bleak. But just as everything came to a head . . . the Holy Spirit began to shed light on what had happened to us and hit Jamie squarely on the forehead with a dose of reality. If he did not immediately cease everything he was doing, he would lose his marriage, his children, his military career, and, most importantly, his soul."

Dawn credits a Protestant chaplain with the question that put a spotlight on the problem: "So, what type of birth control are you all using?" When Jamie described his vasectomy, the chaplain commented, "So, you set yourselves up to fail." Step by step, the couple spent several pain-filled weeks gaining a full understanding of the chaplain's comment and began to seek the counsel of a Catholic priest. In 2005, Jamie underwent a vasectomy reversal, and they had another child.

For some, sexual infidelity is an "unpardonable sin," the choice that will inevitably lead to divorce. And yet, even if we were not the best at always practicing our faith, we probably have heard numerous times how we can't be forgiven by God unless we forgive. "But if you do not forgive others, neither will your Father forgive your trespasses" (Mt 6:15).

Forgiveness is the healthier choice all around. One of the first studies regarding the connection between forgiveness, healing, and health was a survey published in 2001 in the *Journal of Adult Development*. This study found that participants age forty-five and older who practiced forgiveness were more likely to have reported better physical and mental health than those who hung on to wounds from the past. Subsequent studies show that replacing feelings of anger and resentment with mercy and empathy can go so far as to even stop or reverse the stress and strain that comes from anger related to unforgiveness.

While infidelity can shake the bedrock of a marriage, sometimes even the small things can add up and cause lingering resentment in a way that can do real harm to a marriage. Sometimes after doing or saying something that would have previously led to an issue or argument, Dominick and I will say to each other, "What was really so difficult before?" We are blessed with so much—most importantly, with each other.

Yet prior to finding our way back into the arms of Christ, true and deep forgiveness was a rarity. We would say "I'm sorry" and try to move on, but deep down we were keeping score. I would be mad at Dom, for example, for having to go into the office on Saturdays as he was moving up the corporate ladder, even though I had no problem working late almost every night of the week. Dom was often mad at me for not being able to discuss anything beyond what was happening in the newsroom. On the other hand, my job was so stressful that I expected him to understand that when I came home I just needed to vent—even if venting meant ignoring personal matters on the home front. The resentment grew deeper and we grew further and further apart. The tension in our lives was so evident that even our relatives began to notice. Eventually, the friction between us became so unbearable that I decided to call a local hotel home for a few weeks. But, thanks be to God, we never took the final plunge of divorce.

Why not? Maybe it was our Italian Catholic upbringing; we were raised to believe that you don't give up on family. No doubt the Holy Spirit was also at work, speaking to both of our hearts. In any case, bit by bit we made our way back to God. We started actually right back where our marriage began: in a Catholic church—or, to be more precise, in the church's confessional.

We said "yes" again to our marriage by saying "yes" to forgiveness. The merciful balm eased the tensions. The scabs fell off, and old wounds were eventually healed.

While a nice vacation on a warm tropical beach feels great for a little while, nothing will cure what ails the aching heart like a good dose of forgiveness.

Dominick

"I forgive you. I set you free. You don't owe me anything anymore." This was the ending of a powerful story related to me by a dear friend of ours, Deacon Bob Ovies. It was based on the true story of a young girl who had suffered abuse much of her life and came to accept the personal love of Jesus. Her final act of redemption was to forgive her abusers—to set them free and, most importantly, to set herself free.

Only by the grace of God are we able to forgive those who hurt us, perhaps especially those we love. Speaking from personal experience, I can tell you that in the middle of the storm, forgiving the person who has hurt you may very well be the last thing on your mind. You just want to stop hurting and move on. And yet, only after you have stopped keeping score and offered the olive branch can you experience that healing, freeing feeling. Forgiveness sets both parties free so that there can be true reconciliation and so that a more intimate, loving relationship can be realized.

For a good part of our marriage Teresa and I had the dynamic of forgiveness and reconciliation backward. We were constantly trying to reconcile over one thing or another before we truly forgave each other. So instead of forgiving and then coming together to understand each other better, we were trying to convince each other that one of us was right and one of us was wrong. Progress in our relationship was rarely made; we just went on keeping score.

Jesus shows us forgiveness comes first. "While we were still sinners Christ died for us" (Rom 5:8). He didn't wait for us to get our act together or wait until we apologized first. In the midst of our battle with him because of our sin, he forgave us. In the midst of our marriage struggles, we need to forgive first and then seek the healing of reconciliation. It's not that we shouldn't have meaningful dialogue when issues arise, but if we don't start with a heart of forgiveness we will wind up jockeying for our position instead of healing.

Several years ago, Teresa and I were on a Marriage Encounter weekend, still trying to put together some of the last pieces of what had been earlier a shattered marriage. There were still many unresolved issues of who did what to whom, when, what, and why. The last night of the retreat, alone in the quiet of our room, through the grace of the Holy Spirit, we finally turned the corner when we flat-out forgave each other for all the wrongs and hurts without the whys and the wherefores. We didn't say much after that; there wasn't much that needed to be said. But I can still remember the healing and the warmth of that weekend like it was yesterday. Our marriage was never the same after that, thanks be to God.

Forgiving isn't giving the other person the right to do it again or a condoning of the wrong. Forgiveness is a priceless gift God makes available to us to share with each other, allowing us to grow in our mutual relationships. He makes it possible in the first place because he first loved us and set us free. On our own we could never be able to forgive the deep hurts that many of us may have suffered. It's not always easy; it's not always quick to be able to heal, but true forgiveness of a wrong may actually yield a stronger marriage than if the wrong never happened in the first place. God gives us a way to grow stronger in spite of adversity when we call on his grace to empower us to forgive and to soothe each other's wounds.

Tips for Willing Forgiveness

Is your marriage in an unending cycle of who did what to whom, and when, and how? Do you want to break free from this cycle and experience the liberating feeling of unconditional love and forgiveness? Here are some steps you can take to practice this spiritual work of mercy that will bring healing and newfound love to you both.

Take a look at how you have contributed to the problem. Jesus tells us to pull the plank out of our own eye before we point to the speck in our brother's eye. Go to confession and ask God for the strength to forgive and love your spouse unconditionally. Then talk to your spouse about the hurt you may have knowingly or unknowingly caused. Ask for their forgiveness and discuss ways to prevent those hurts from happening in the future.

Are you struggling to find forgiveness in your heart for something your spouse has done to you or your family? If you are having a hard time forgiving your spouse, think about a time in your life outside of your marriage where someone—maybe a parent, a friend, or a sibling—forgave you for a wrong you committed. Examine how that forgiveness made you feel. Taking an honest look at your own forgiveness experience can often make it easier for you to do the same.

Together, take a look at what the scriptures have to say about forgiveness. In order to gain a deeper understanding of our responsibility to forgive, sit down together and read and then discuss the following scripture passages:

- Matthew 6:14–15
- 1 John 1:9
- Acts 3:19
- Isaiah 1:18

Prayer for the Forgiving and Forgiven

Lord, you tell us that we are fearfully and wonderfully made, because we are made in your image and likeness. You know us better than we know ourselves. You know what's best for us. Open our minds and hearts continually to the power of forgiveness, and give us the strength to be the first to say "I'm sorry." Amen.

Reflection Questions

1. Make a list of all the things you need to forgive—and all that you need forgiveness for. Circle the things on your list you or your spouse have done that you are unable to forgive. What do you think is blocking the pathway to forgiveness?

2. Saint John Paul II said, "Forgiveness is not the opposite of justice." What do you think this means? Could it be that you fear forgiveness will mean justice won't be served in some way?

3. Are you having a hard time forgiving yourself? How might this be affecting your marriage, and how can your spouse help you truly embrace your identity as a loved son or daughter of God?

Thirteen

Comfort the Afflicted

Help your spouse deal with stress.

IIIIIIIIIIIIIIIIIIIIIIIIIIIIIIIIIIIIIIIIIIIIIIIIIIIIIIIIIIIIIIIIIIIIIIIIIIIIIIIIIIIIIIIIIIIIIIIIIIIIIIIIIIIIIIIIIIIIIIII

Always and ever . . . now and forever
Little things mean a lot.

—*Edith Lindeman, "Little Things Mean a Lot"*

Teresa

Ah, stress: the gift that keeps on giving. Even if you've been pretty good at applying forbearance and forgiveness in your marriage, let's face it—life still happens. As one of my favorite *Saturday Night Live* characters Roseanne Roseannadanna used to say, "It's always somethin'. If it isn't one thing, it's another."

Today's busy married couples could all probably star in their own three-ring circus, as they are among the best jugglers and acrobats on the planet, handling multiple tasks and performing some pretty amazing balancing routines—especially when you bring active children into the mix. It's no wonder national statistics show that today's married couples only spend on average four minutes alone together each day. It's an alarming statistic; but then again, maybe not so alarming if we all stop and do a quick assessment of our daily to-do lists. Think of how much time is spent at work as well as shuttling children back and forth to school, doctor appointments, and soccer practice. And this is before we even take a look at the hours involved in running a household, between the cooking, cleaning, walking the dog, and doing the grocery shopping. The four-minute figure actually makes sense when we zoom out and examine the big picture of our jam-packed lives.

Two friends of ours, Rich and Fran, remember a time when the stresses of their lives affected them very differently as individuals—and also drastically weakened their marriage. Before Fran met Rich, she had been diagnosed with a severe autoimmune disease, myasthenia gravis, and her father had told her she'd "be lucky to find someone to marry" her. It greatly affected her self-esteem and made her feel like a burden to her family. Yet when she met Rich at a costume party, she knew God had answered her prayers. They were engaged a year later and married a year after that. "I felt unconditional love from Rich," Fran recalls. "And within five years, I went into remission." They were blessed with three children in the first ten years of marriage.

Unfortunately, Rich struggled to provide for his growing family and soon turned to betting on horse races, coming home later and later at night. When Fran confronted Rich about his gambling, he tried to justify it. "I don't hunt, or go to bars, or play golf. This is my hobby." Later, he commented, "Nagging is worse than being nibbled to death by a duck." In time, Fran was able to persuade Rich to go with her to a Marriage Encounter weekend so they could learn new ways to communicate. Grudgingly, he went.

"I continued to struggle with gambling," Rich recalls. "It was like walking on a tightrope, trying to satisfy my family's needs and my own desire to gamble. I tried to control Fran and manipulate her because I wanted to have my own way. At the same time, I was depressed. I knew I needed to change and that I did not want to lose Fran's love. When a man invited me to a men's prayer group, I confessed my gambling addiction. That group of men kept me accountable, and eventually I stopped all forms of gambling."

What was it that helped them to rebuild? "Once, at a World Marriage Day dinner," Rich remembers, "Deacon Bob Ovies spoke on praying together as a couple. We heard that for couples who regularly attend church and pray together, less than 2 percent divorce. That brought us to our knees, seeking God's will for our lives. It brought a unity in our marriage we never had before."

What are some of the things they wish they'd done differently, in retrospect? Fran wonders if she did the right thing getting a job that took her out of the home after Rich's company went on strike. "It caused our lives to be chaotic, and our son needed more of our time." But they both acknowledge that, because of his gambling, the need was real.

Rich, on the other hand, deeply regrets the harsh words he used with his wife and children during that time of his life. "I cannot take those words back, and I wish I hadn't overreacted so much."

Most of all, they both wish that they had sought and prayed for God's will early on. "We often made our own decisions, then asked God to help us make them work out," Fran said. "Now we realize that God has a plan for our marriage . . . just as he has a plan for yours."

Do you ever feel as though you are starring in your own Barnum and Bailey number and are working without a net? Is stress overtaking your life? If so, how do you cope with the stressors? When we think of that safety net, it often comes in the form of a big-ticket item: a vacation, a weekend away, or a marriage retreat. These are all good things, but a weekend or a vacation in and of itself without follow-up is not going to produce long-lasting results. Eventually you have to come back to reality, down off the mountaintop, and learn how to live and love to the fullest each and every day.

That's why we believe that good things—very good things—come in small packages delivered daily to help us with the messiness of stress. Since I write, speak, and host a daily talk show as well as cohost a syndicated Catholic TV show, I am constantly on a deadline. I work great under pressure. That comes from thirty-plus years of doing live radio and TV. But even with more than three decades of experience, sometimes all the deadlines can come together seemingly at once. That's enough to drive even the most seasoned multitasker nuts.

I can always count on Dom to make the stressful periods . . . well, less stressful. Whether it's bringing me a cup of hot tea if I am working late into the evening or making sure the coffee is ready to go when I get up a little earlier in the morning to get some writing done, he is showing me he cares. I swear I can actually feel my shoulders relaxing and my heart rate slowing down just by hearing my husband proclaim some of my favorite words in the English language: "Dinner's ready" or "I just threw in a load of whites." These words can be just as romantic and meaningful as "I love you" and "I miss you." When Dom says these things to me, I know he is doing whatever he can to make the stressful times less stressful. Often I will come home and walk into the house to find roses from his garden on the kitchen table or on the desk in my office. He'll also manage to send me sweet messages via text or e-mail, complete with photos of some of our favorite towns from our favorite place to visit: Italy.

Maybe it's because we have been down the hectic, stop-the-world-I-want-to-get-off road before. We know where that road can lead when we don't help each other deal with the crazy busyness of life along the way. When it comes to helping each other deal with stress, little things, as the old song says, do indeed mean a lot.

Dominick

It was July 4, 1988. Although it was a holiday, I had to go to work. I was in the middle of a huge assignment, and I was way behind and had been working seven days a week for several weeks. This was, at the time, one of the biggest challenges I had in my career. To say I was stressed out wasn't even in the ballpark. I had never been in a position like this before and, because it was relatively early in my career, I didn't know how to handle the stress.

Fortunately, my wife did. That morning, I angrily walked into the kitchen to grab a quick breakfast with Teresa and head out the door. I was feeling frustrated that I had to work on a holiday in the middle of the summer, our favorite time of year.

When I walked into the kitchen, there was my wife looking like the Statue of Liberty, wearing a silly-looking crown with a paper torch in her right hand, dressed in a blue shirt and shorts. On the table were red, white, and blue breakfast treats. I was totally surprised, and I chuckled, asking what this was all about, but I knew the answer. What I remember most about that day was both her broad smile and the little tear in her eye. She was showing me how much she loved me by helping me deal with stress and at the same time trying hard not to let me see how bad she felt for me, which only served to show me her love even more.

There has been a lot of water under the bridge in our marriage since that day, but Teresa was truly being Christ for me and meeting me where I was, trying to lift me up and out of where I was. Neither of us would have articulated that incident in that particular way. God was working in our lives, helping us to help each other with the everyday trials and temptations, the importance of which can be easily dismissed or downplayed in our marriages.

Managing stress can be one of the best things we can do to increase our overall health and well-being, and there are many ways to do this: exercise, meditation, and breathing techniques are all good places to start. The thing with stress is that we often don't recognize it in ourselves because it typically builds bit by bit. The person under stress often lashes out at those closest to him, hurting the ones he loves. And for me, the last thing I wanted to hear was how stressed I was, how I needed to calm down, or to get a grip. And that's exactly what Teresa *didn't* do on July 4, 1988. She turned to one of her God-given strengths—joyfulness—and understanding my needs, she was able to break through the grip of stress I was feeling.

On the flip side, when Teresa is stressed, the last thing she needs is one of my strong points: problem solving. She would much rather I listen and affirm her feelings. Although I am always tempted to jump in and offer solutions, over the years God has shown me that meeting people where they are establishes a connection with them first, and understanding their needs and responding to their needs is what is most important.

During a diaconate internship in hospice care one summer, one of the people I visited was an elderly curmudgeon named Rudy. Every time my internship supervisor and I went into his room, he was never in a good mood. Talking with him was difficult. I really did everything I could think of to try to connect with Rudy. I spoke with him about his prayer life, about God, asked about how he was feeling; but I never felt that my words were reaching him. One day we were about to leave and he said something about not having a working television. So I picked up the remote, pushed a few buttons, fiddled with the buttons on the TV and, voilà, the television came on.

Funny thing: Rudy's entire demeanor changed. His face was beaming with delight. As we walked out of his room I heard him tell the nurse, "Hey, I like that guy." Rudy couldn't do for himself what he wanted, and his stress I am sure was building. But God put me there that day just so I could fix the TV remote. As husband and wife, God has put you together to similarly help each other with the stress of life. This includes all major challenges, such as a heavy workload, or a frustrating TV remote.

Tips to Comfort the Afflicted

No two couples experience the same kind of stressors, and no two individuals handle stress in exactly the same way. Learning to recognize stress and provide a comforting response is one of the most important ways to be a source of intimate grace for the one you love. And the best time to figure out how to meet your spouse's needs in this area is not in the middle of the crisis but before it hits. Here are a few tips to help you make a plan for "comfort care."

Think about ways your spouse has helped you deal with stress. Share with each other what those efforts have meant during particularly difficult times. Whether it's picking up the dry cleaning, ordering carryout, or planning that weekend alone, don't be afraid to suggest other ideas on how to help each other live a more stress-free marriage.

Identify the areas of your life that are most prone to stressful reactions. Sit down together and take some time to think about the most stressful areas of your life. Discuss how you can possibly ease each other's burdens.

Examine your routines to see if there are things you could both be doing to alleviate stress in your own lives. Examine the ways you tend to relieve stress and make sure they are healthy activities that don't take time away from your most important relationships: with God, with each other, and with your children. Work on incorporating stress relievers, such as exercise, together. Take a walk. Go for a bike ride.

Prayer for the Stressed

Jesus, you told your disciples, "Peace I give you; peace I leave with you." We pray that we are always able to take that extra step to bring more true peace and less stress into our lives. Amen.

Reflection Questions

1. How can you tell when your spouse is feeling stressed? What behavioral clues have you noticed? Are you aware of your spouse's stress level and what causes it to increase or decrease?

2. Do you regularly sit down as a couple and examine how you share day-to-day responsibilities: housework, meal preparation, child care, after-school and work activities, paperwork? Do you feel there is a balance here, or does there need to be some adjusting so one partner isn't carrying most of the load?

3. How often do the two of you "retreat" from the daily grind and spend some time alone together? When was the last time you and your spouse took some time out just for the two of you, away from the everyday hustle and bustle? (If it's been a while, why not start making plans right now?)

Fourteen

Pray for the Living and the Dead

Tap into the power of thankful, persistent intercession.

Don't pray when you feel like it. Have an appointment with the Lord and keep it. A man is powerful on his knees.

—*Corrie ten Boom*

Teresa

If you could find one pill that would drastically decrease your odds of getting divorced, wouldn't you run to the nearest CVS or Walgreens and grab as much of the product as humanly possible? That's what happens when couples consistently pray together in good times and in bad. Studies over the past thirty years have shown that couples who practiced faith-based activities together—such as daily prayer, scripture reading, or attending church together—do experience a much lower divorce rate, with one study showing a divorce rate of fewer than one in 1,105 marriages among couples who pray together daily.[1] Other research, including a 2010 report by Florida State University, found that prayer can even help couples steer clear of infidelity.[2]

Just like people, prayer comes in many shapes and sizes. Some couples may enjoy incorporating more formal prayer into their routines, such as daily Mass and/or the Rosary. Others prefer to pray more spontaneously by just holding hands and talking out loud to God together. Our dear friends Julie and Greg Alexander have some great ideas on couple prayer, and you'll find information about their ministry in our resource section. However or whenever you decide to do it, just keep praying—even if it's only for a few minutes each day.

Years ago, after Dom and I came back to the Church, we decided our daily form of prayer would come through the daily Mass readings. We tried doing them at night, but that didn't work because Dom tends to fall asleep the minute his head hits the pillow. Dinner also wasn't the greatest option, since due to our busy work schedules we often got home too late or had other outside commitments. We found that reading the scriptures together before we head off to work in the morning has been very doable for us. We began that practice twenty-two years ago and still manage to do this almost every day of the week.

Reading the Bible for us has special meaning, because it was through a Bible study that we first found our way back to God and the Catholic Church. We use a daily Catholic devotional that includes the Mass readings, a reflection, and a prayer. I have lost track of how often the readings have pertained directly to something that was happening in our lives. Sometimes the affirmations from God are so obvious we have to laugh out loud. It's as if Jesus moved around the particular scripture verses that day just to say, "Hey, I hear you." And he does indeed. The readings also provide a great opportunity to learn more about our faith and each other. We talk about what the verse means to us or about what the Church has to say about applying the verses to our lives.

Setting the prayer time for the same time each day has made a difference in the ability to keep it up for so long. It is just part of our daily routine. As a deacon, Dom is required to pray the Liturgy of the Hours, the daily prayers required for all priests and deacons in the Catholic Church. I also use another Catholic devotional that includes morning and evening prayer. Even when we are doing prayer on our own, we somehow feel connected or closer to each other.

We have kept this prayer activity going in good times and in bad. It's spawned more spontaneous prayer than we expected—thanking God for healing our marriage and giving us so many blessings. It has brought us great peace in difficult times, including the deaths of both of our fathers in the last few years. It makes it so much easier to talk about the most important relationships in our lives: our relationship with Christ and with each other. And it all started with just a few minutes a day.

We're so glad you took time out of your busy life to read *Intimate Graces*. God saved our marriage, and like the Alexanders and the other real-life couples you met in these pages, we know he can not only save yours but also make it the best it can be. That's why I can't think of a better way to end this book than with a chapter that I hope will help you start praying together. Christian writer Corrie ten Boom was right: a man is powerful on his knees. So is a married couple.

Dominick

When we were first married, about the only praying Teresa and I did was a quick grace before meals. Praying as a couple, even after we came back to the Church, was not something that seemed to come naturally; maybe we shouldn't expect it to.

I think the best way Satan can break down a marriage is to prevent or distract a couple from communicating with each other and with God, individually and as a couple. When Teresa and I were dating and first married, it was amazing how long we could talk with each other about all sorts of things. Now, if you know my wife, that's not exactly a shock. But I am not the most loquacious person in the world, so that is why I always thought communication was our greatest asset. But lack of a strong faith and a practically nonexistent prayer life combined with a long list of other issues led to our marriage hitting some pretty tough times. What was once our greatest asset became our biggest failing; we no longer could communicate on any level.

Long story short, the Lord came back into our lives in a profoundly unexpected way, and eventually we fell in love again—with each other, with Jesus, and with our Catholic faith. We discovered the joy of each other, a Church that had two thousand years of history behind it but was still relevant today, and, most importantly, we rediscovered Jesus. He became a Jesus who was real and personal, someone we could talk to and with. Saint Teresa of Avila said that prayer is nothing more than an intimate conversation between friends. Paradoxically, prayer doesn't always come easily, and each of us has his own style and spirituality. For example, I am more formal in my approach; Teresa is more familiar in hers. Nonetheless, prayer is the glue that helps us stay connected in good times and in bad.

As Teresa mentioned, one of the forms of daily prayer that we enjoy most is reading scripture together, in particular the daily Mass readings. Whatever form of prayer you choose, you will find that in prayer a husband and wife lift each other up to Jesus, presenting each other to him, trusting in him for his mercy. There is no greater gift we can give our spouses than to lift them up in prayer. Praying not only brings us into closer contact with Jesus but also with each other; even if I am praying alone in my room, I feel intimately connected to Teresa.

In his messages of divine mercy to Saint Faustina, the Lord continually stressed trust in his mercy to heal and forgive. When we make prayer a part of our marriage routine, we are trusting in God to respond to the needs we present to him, albeit in his way and in his time. It's our affirmation to him that we understand he is really in control of our lives. He is the one who strengthens us to do all the worthwhile things we are doing in our lives: raising a family, holding a job, caring for aging parents. All these things have real consequence in this world and can be a source of daily delight and challenge. We need God's strength to get it all done.

Praying in thanksgiving for the delights and with the trust for mercy in the challenges is one of the best ways we can flourish in our marriages. No man or woman is an island. We need each other and we need God's mercy and love. Prayer opens our hearts to know Jesus and to grow closer to each other. When we bring the needs and concerns of our hearts to Jesus, as a couple, he transforms us both so that every day we can be more and more like Jesus toward our spouse, especially in those moments he or she most needs to experience such intimate grace.

Some good friends of ours years ago gave us a great mental picture about couple prayer. They said think of God at the apex of a triangle and each of us at the two other corners of the triangle. When we pray as a couple, we ascend the sides of the triangle and two things happen: we get closer to the apex as in God and we draw closer to each other. The goal, after all—not only in couple prayer but also in our marriage—is to arrive at the top, together as one with God.

Tips for Praying for the Longevity of Your Marriage

Sit down together with this book and discuss what types of prayer experiences you've tried in the past, and what you might like to try to bring this part of your marriage back to life! In addition to the Couple Prayer series mentioned in the resource section, you might also try daily devotionals such as *Sacred Reading* (Ave Maria Press), *Magnificat*, *Word Among Us*, or *Give Us This Day*. Make a commitment to set aside a few minutes a day to pray. It might feel awkward at first, but keep trying.

Talk about how you can incorporate couple prayer into your daily life. Consider your schedules and try to come up with a realistic plan that would help make prayer a regular part of your routine.

If you've never prayed together before, be patient and persistent. Try different times and approaches until you find one that works for you. Try praying silently while holding hands, journaling your prayers, or try reading a psalm or other scripture passage slowly and reflectively.

Don't put too much pressure on yourself. If spontaneous prayer is not your thing, then start with a formula prayer such as the Hail Mary or the Lord's Prayer. Then, after you say those prayers together, ask God out loud to bless your spouse and take turns telling God what you love about your spouse.

Start a conversation about prayer by recalling a prayer that was answered, whether recent or in the past.

Prayer for a New Life Together

Lord, you promised that when two or more are gathered in your name, there you are also. We ask you to guide us as we do our best to incorporate more prayer and more of you into our lives. We trust this small effort will reap great rewards and that our marriage will be blessed more than we could ever imagine. Amen.

Reflection Questions

1. How have you seen the power of prayer at work in your life, your marriage, and your family?

2. How often do you pray, both individually and as a couple? Are you satisfied with the level of prayer in your own life as well as in your marriage and family?

3. How do you think persistent prayer has helped your marriage or other marriages you know?

4. The last work of mercy is "pray for the living and the dead." What areas of your life together do you see as "alive," a source of thanksgiving and happiness? What areas do you think have "died" and need to be revived? Commit to praying together for a fresh outpouring of "intimate grace" in your life together. God always answers the prayers of those who want to grow in perfect love!

Appendix
Resources to Help You

‖‖

Ministries to Married Couples

The Alexander House, founded by Greg and Julie Alexander, offers many resources for hurting couples as well as for those who just want to nurture their marriages. For more information, go to www.thealexanderhouse.org.

Retrouvaille: Couples who experience significant difficulty in their marriages—because of circumstances within the marriage or from stressors outside the relationship—can receive support and practical assistance in rebuilding their relationship. (*Retrouvaille* is French for "rediscovery.") For more information, visit www.retrouvaille.org.

Worldwide Marriage Encounter: This Catholic marriage-enrichment program offers married couples a life-changing opportunity to look deeply at their relationship with each other and with God over the course of a weekend retreat (www.wwme.org).

National Marriage Encounter: This Christian program is hosted across the country in a series of weekend events that help married couples cultivate and deepen their relationship through open and honest communication, both with each other and with other Christian couples. Go to marriage-encounter.org for more information.

Multimedia Resources for Parish or Home Use

Beloved is a unique program of marriage preparation and enrichment featuring twelve video sessions on six DVDs, a collaboration of the Augustine Institute, Ignatius Press, and Lighthouse Catholic Media. For more information, go to lighthousecatholicmedia.org/beloved.

Marriage: Unique for a Reason is an initiative of the United States Conference of Catholic Bishops. This video and study guide explores the meaning of marriage and the unique role it plays in society. Available in both English and Spanish, this resource is available through marriage-uniqueforareason.org.

Together for Life Online is a marriage-preparation and enrichment outreach of Ave Maria Press designed to support young couples preparing for and beginning their life together as married couples. For more information, go to togetherforlifeonline.com.

Together with Jesus **Couple Prayer Series** by Bob and Kathy Ovies. This six-week DVD-based series helps married couples more fully enjoy the life-changing intimacy that comes from praying together. Visit coupleprayer.com.

Books and Other Resources

CovenantEyes is an online accountability program to help those who are tempted by pornography (www.covenant eyes.com). If someone you love is struggling with pornography, pick up a copy of Bishop Paul Loverde's pastoral letter "Bought with a Price" (www.arlingtondiocese.org/ purity/index.aspx).

Familiaris Consortio (On the Role of the Christian Family in the Modern World) by Saint John Paul II may be found online at the Vatican website, w2.vatican.va/content/john-paul-ii/en/apost_exhortations/documents/hf_jp-ii_exh_19811122_familiaris-consortio.html.

Marriage 9-1-1: How God Saved Our Marriage (and Can Save Yours, Too!) by Greg and Julie Alexander. In this book, Greg and Julie share the story of how God intervened in their lives at a time when their marriage was on the rocks, and how other couples can experience this same kind of divine intervention in their lives. Order at www.amazon. com/Marriage-911-Saved-Save-Yours/dp/0867169796.

Sacred Reading by the Apostleship of Prayer (Ave Maria Press). Refresh your marriage with scripture! Pick up a copy of this annual daily reader from the Apostleship of Prayer, the "pope's prayer group," and let God speak to your hearts from the daily Gospels.

Notes

Foreword

1. In her book *The Good News about Marriage,* Shaunti Feldhahn reports findings from an eight-year study that reveals that the divorce rate among those who attend church regularly is significantly lower. One article in *Western Journalism* quotes Feldhahn's assertion that the rate of divorce among practicing Christians is between "27 and 50 percent lower than among non-churchgoers" (Matt Barber, "You May Have Heard That the Divorce Rate in the Church Is 50% . . . Get Ready to Be Shocked" *Western Journalism,* August 21, 2014, accessed July 13, 2015, www.westernjournal ism.com/flash-christians-actually-far-less-likely-divorce).

1. Feed the Hungry

1. Pope Francis, "Visit to the Community of Varginha," July 25, 2013, accessed March 4, 2015, http://w2.vatican.va/content/francesco/en/speeches/2013/july/documents/papa-francesco_20130725_gmg-comunita-varginha.html. Emphasis added.

2. United States Conference of Catholic Bishops, "Marriage FAQs," *Marriage: Unique for a Reason,* accessed March 4, 2015, www.marriageuniqueforareason.org/faq/#sec1q3.

3. Clothe the Naked

1. Anne-Marie Slaughter, "Why Women Still Can't Have It All," *The Atlantic,* June 13, 2012, accessed March 4,

2015, www.theatlantic.com/magazine/archive/2012/07/why-women-still-cant-have-it-all/309020.

7. Bury the Dead

1. Buzz Cason and Tom Douglas, "Love's the Only House," from the album *Emotion*, produced and performed by Martina McBride (1999, RCA Nashville), CD single.

8. Instruct the Ignorant

1. Pope John Paul II, World Youth Day, 1993. Denver, Colorado.

10. Admonish the Sinner

1. Amy E. Bonomi, Julianna M. Nemeth, Lauren E. Altenburger, Melissa L. Anderson, Anastasia Snyder, and Irma Dotto, "Fiction or Not? Fifty Shades Is Associated with Health Risks in Adolescent and Young Adult Females," *Journal of Women's Health* September 2014, 23(9): 720–728.

14. Pray for the Living and the Dead

1. *Retrouvaille International Handbook*, 2005, as quoted on www.coupleprayer.com.

2. Frank D. Fincham and Nathaniel M. Lambert, "Faith and Unfaithfulness: Can Praying for Your Partner Reduce Infidelity?" *Journal of Personality and Social Psychology* 2010, 99(4): 649–659), http://fincham.info/papers/2010-jpsp-prayer.pdf.

Ordained a deacon in the Archdiocese of Detroit in 2012, **Dominick Pastore** ministers to couples at retreats, pilgrimages, conferences. He serves as a deacon at St. Angela and St. Isaac Jogues churches in suburban Detroit. Pastore has a master's degree in pastoral studies from Sacred Heart Major Seminary in Detroit.

He is vice president and senior electrical engineer for SmithGroupJJR in Detroit, where he's been employed since 1980. Pastore is a knight in the Order of Malta, and member of the board of Mary's Mantle, a Catholic home for pregnant and unwed mothers. He and his wife, Teresa Tomeo, lead pilgrimages to Rome and other parts of Italy for married couples.

Teresa Tomeo is a bestselling author, syndicated Catholic talk show host, and speaker with more than thirty years of experience in print and broadcast media. Her weekday radio program, *Catholic Connection*, a coproduction of Ave Maria Radio and EWTN, is heard daily on 300 stations nationwide and also SiriusXM Satellite Radio. Her TV show, *The Catholic View for Women*, is seen twice weekly on EWTN.

Tomeo is a columnist and special correspondent for *Our Sunday Visitor*. She has been featured on *The O'Reilly Factor*, *Fox News*, *Fox and Friends*, MSNBC, and the *Dr. Laura Show*. She was named a Vatican conference speaker and conference delegate and spoke at the 2013 conference the "Rights of the Family and the Challenges of the Contemporary World" sponsored by the Pontifical Council for the Family. Tomeo participated in the Vatican Women's Congress in 2008. She speaks throughout North America and also leads retreats and pilgrimages annually. Tomeo is a teacher for St. Benedict Press's Catholic Courses. Her books include *Extreme Makeover*, *God's Bucket List*, and *Walk Softly and Carry and Great Bag*. She and her husband, Dominick Pastore, live in St. Clair Shores, Michigan.